THE
ADVENTURES

OF

JOHN JEWITT

ONLY SURVIVOR OF THE CREW OF THE SHIP

BOSTON

DURING A CAPTIVITY OF NEARLY THREE YEARS

AMONG THE

INDIANS OF NOOTKA SOUND

IN VANCOUVER ISLAND

EDITED

WITH AN INTRODUCTION AND NOTES

BY

ROBERT BROWN, Ph.D., M.A., F.L.S.

COMMANDER OF THE FIRST VANCOUVER EXPLORING EXPEDITION

WITH THIRTEEN ILLUSTRATIONS

CLEMENT WILSON

29 PATERNOSTER ROW, LONDON, E.C.

1896

[All Rights Reserved]

with kind regards of

W. W. Brown

IN MEMORY

A SAD interest attaches to this little book. Although published after his death, and therefore deprived of his final revision, it was not the last work which Dr. Robert Brown did. His manuscript was actually completed many months ago, but at his own request it was returned to him to receive a last careful overhaul at his hands. This revision had been practically finished, and the MS. lay ready uppermost among the papers in his desk, where it was found after his death. Dr. Brown died on the morning of the 26th of October, 1895, working almost to his last hour. Before the leader he had written for the *Standard* on the evening of the 25th had come under the eyes of its readers, the hand that had penned it was cold in death. Between the evening and the morning he went home. He was only fifty-three, but "a righteous man, though he die before his time, shall be at rest."

And in one sense Dr. Brown needed rest—ay, even this last and sweetest rest of all. His life had been one of unremitting work—work well done, which the busy, hurrying world mostly heeded not, knowing naught of the hand that did it. Some twenty years ago, when I first knew him, he was a fair, stalwart Northerner, full of vigour, mirthful also, and apparently looking out on the voyage of life with the confident, joyous eye of one who

ADVENTURES OF JOHN JEWITT.

——◆——

INTRODUCTION

MANY years ago—when America was in the midst of war, when railways across the continent were but the dream of sanguine men, and when the Pacific was a far-away sea—the writer of these lines passed part of a pleasant summer in cruising along the western shores of Vancouver Island. Our ship's company was not distinguished, for it consisted of two fur-traders and an Indian "boy," and the sloop in which the crew and passengers sailed was so small, that, when the wind failed, and the brown folk ashore looked less amiable and the shore more rugged than was desirable, we put her and ourselves beyond hail by the aid of what seamen know as a "white ash breeze." Out of one fjord we went, only to enter another so like it that there was often a difficulty in deciding by the mere appearance of the shore which was which. Everywhere the dense forest of Douglas fir and Menzies spruce covered the country from the water's edge to the summit of the rounded hills which here and there caught the eye in the still little known, but at that date almost entirely unexplored interior. Wherever a tree could obtain a foothold, there a tree grew, until in places their roots were at times laved by the spray. Beneath this thick clothing of heavy timber flourished an almost equally dense undergrowth of

DR. BROWN'S "BOY."

shrubs, which until then were only known to us from the specimens introduced from North-West America into the European gardens. Gay were the thickets of thimbleberry [1] and salmonberry [2] wherever the soil was rich, and for miles the ground was carpeted with the salal,[3] while the huckleberry,[4] the crab-apple,[5] and the flowering currant [6] varied the monotony of the gloomy woods. In places the ginseng, or, as the woodmen call it, the "devil's walking-stick,"[7] with its long prickly stem and palm-like

[1] *Rubus Nutkanus.*   [2] *Rubus spectabilis.*   [3] *Gaultheria Shallon.*
[4] *Vaccinium ovatum.*   [5] *Pyrus rivularis.*
[6] *Ribes sanguineum,* now a common shrub in our ornamental grounds.
[7] *Echinopanax horridum.*

head of great leaves, imparted an almost tropical aspect
to scenery which, seen from the deck of our little craft,
looked so like that of Southern Norway, that I have
never seen the latter without recalling the outer limits
of British Columbia. On the few flat spits where the
sun reached, the gigantic cedars[1] and broad-leaved
maples[2] lighted up the scene, while the dogwood,[3] with
its large white flowers reflected in the water of some
river which, after a turbulent course, had reached the sea
through a placid mouth, or a Menzies arbutus,[4] whose
glossy leaves and brown bark presented a more
southern facies to the sombre jungles, afforded here
and there a relief to the never-ending fir and pine and
spruce.

A more solitary shore, so far as white men are
concerned, it would be hard to imagine. From the day
we left until the day we returned, we sighted only one
sail; and from Port San Juan, where an Indian trader
lived a lonely life in an often-beleaguered blockhouse,
to Koskeemo Sound, where another of these voluntary
exiles passed his years among the savages, there was
not a christened man, with the exception of the little
settlement of lumbermen at the head of the Alberni
Canal. For months at a time no keel ever ploughed
this sea, and then too frequently it was a warship sent
from Victoria to chastise the tribesmen for some outrage
committed on wayfaring men such as we. The floating
fur-trader with whom we exchanged the courtesies of
the wilderness had indeed been despitefully used. For

---

[1] *Thuja gigantea*, a tree which to the Indian is what the bamboo is to
the Chinese.

[2] *Acer macrophyllum.*   [3] *Cornus Nuttallii.*   [4] *Arbutus Menziesii.*

had he not taken to himself some savage woman, who had levanted, to her tribe with those miscellaneous effects which he termed "iktas"?   And the Klayoquahts

PORT SAN JUAN INDIANS.

had stolen his boat, and the Kaoquahts his beans and his vermilion and his rice, and threatened to scuttle his schooner and stick his head on its masthead.   And, moreover, to complete this tale of public pillage and private wrong, a certain chief, to whom he applied many ornate epithets, had declared that he cared not a salal-berry for all of "King George's warships." So that the conclusion of this merchant of the wilds was that, until "half the Indians were hanged, and the other half badly licked, there would be no peace on the coast for honest men such as he."   Then, under a cloud of playful blasphemy, our friend sailed away.

For if civilisation was scarce in the Western Vancouver

of '63, savagedom was all-abounding. Not many hours passed without our having dealings with the lords of the soil. It was indeed our business—or, at least, the business of the two men and the Indian "boy"—to meet with and make profit out of the barbarous folk. Hence it was seldom that we went to sleep without the din of a board village in our ears, or woke without the ancient and most fish-like smell of one being the first odour which greeted our nostrils. In almost every cove, creek, or inlet there was one of these camps, and every few miles we entered the territory of a new tribe, ruled by a rival chief, rarely on terms with his neighbour, and as often as not at war with him. More than once we had occasion to witness the gruesome evidence of this state of matters. A war party returning from a raid on a distant hamlet would be met with, all painted in hideous colours, and with the bleeding heads of their decapitated enemies fastened to the bows of their cedar canoes, and the cowering captives, doomed to slavery, bound among the fighting men. Or, casting anchor in front of a village, we would be shown with pride a row of festering skulls stuck on poles, as proof of the military prowess of our shifty hosts.

These were, however, unusually unpleasant incidents. More frequently we saw little except the more lightsome traits of what was then a very primitive savage life, and the barbarous folk treated us kindly. A marriage feast might be in progress, or a great "potlatch," or merry-making, at which the giving away of property was the principal feature (p. 82), might be in full blaze at the very moment we steered round the wooded point. Halibut

2

and dog-fish were being caught in vast quantities—the one for slicing and drying for winter use; the other for the sake of the oil extracted from the liver, then as now an important article of barter, being in ready demand by the Puget Sound saw-mills. Now and then a fur-seal or, better still, a sea-otter would be killed. But this is not the land of choice furs. Even the marten and the mink were indifferent. Beaver—which in those days, after having been almost hunted to death, were again getting numerous, owing to the low prices which the pelts brought having slackened the trappers' zeal—would often be brought on board, and a few hides of the wapiti, the "elk" of the Western hunter, and the black-tailed deer which swarm in the Vancouver woods, generally appeared at every village. The natives are, however, essentially fish-eaters, and though in every tribe there is generally a hunter or two, the majority of them seldom wander far afield, the interior being in their mythology a land of evil things, of which wise men would do well to keep clear. Even the black bear, which in autumn was often a common feature of the country, where it ranged the crab-apple thickets, was not at this season an object of the chase. Like the deer and the wolves, it was shunning the heat and the flies by summering near the snow which we could notice still capping some of the inland hills, rising to heights of from five thousand to seven thousand feet, and feasting on the countless salmon which were descending every stream, until, with the receding waters, they were left stranded in the upland pools. So cheap were salmon, that at times they could be bought for a cent's worth of "trade goods," and deer in winter for a few

charges of powder and shot. A whale-hunt, in which
the behemoth was attacked by harpoons with attached
inflated sealskins, after a fashion with which I had
become familiar when a resident among the Eskimo
of Baffin Bay, was a more curious sight. Yet dog-fish
oil was the staple of the unpicturesque traffic in which
my companions engaged ; while I, a hunter after less
considered trifles, landed to roam the woods and shores
for days at a time, gathering the few flowers which
bloomed under these umbrageous forests, though in
number sufficient to tempt the red-beaked humming-
bird[1] to migrate from Mexico to these northern regions,
its tiny nest being frequently noticed on the tops of
low bushes.

But, after all, the most interesting sight on the shore
was the people who inhabited it. They
were the " Indians," whom my friend Gilbert
Sproat afterwards described as the " Ahts,"[2] for this
syllable terminates the name of each of the many
little tribes into which they are divided. Yet, with
a disregard of the laws of nomenclature, the Ethno-
logical Bureau at Washington has only recently
announced its intention of knowing them officially by
the meaningless title of " Wakashan." They are a
people by themselves, speaking a language which
was confined to Vancouver Island, with the exception
of Cape Flattery, the western tip of Washington, where
the Makkahs speak it. In Vancouver Island, a region

The Aht Indians

---

[1] *Selasphorus rufus.* It is one of one hundred and fifty-three birds which
I catalogued from Vancouver Island (*Ibis*, Nov. 1868.)

[2] *Scenes and Studies of Savage Life* (1868), by the Hon. G. M.
Sproat, late Commissioner of Indian Affairs for British Columbia.

about the size of Ireland, three, if not four distinct
aboriginal tongues are in use, in addition to Chinook
Jargon, a sort of *lingua franca* employed by the Indians
in their intercourse with the whites or with tribes
whose speech they do not understand. The Kawitshen
(Cowitchan) with its various dialects, the chief of which is
the Tsongersth (Songer) of the people near Victoria,
prevails from Sooke in the Strait of Juan de Fuca,
northwards to Comox. From that point to the northern
end of the island various dialects of the Kwakiool
(Cogwohl of the traders) are the medium in which the
tribesmen do not conceal their thoughts. The people of
Quatseno and Koskeemo Sounds, owing to their frequent
intercourse with Fort Rupert on the other side of the
island, which at this point is at its narrowest, understand and frequently speak the Kwakiool. But after
passing several days entirely alone among these people, I
can vouch for the fact that this dialect is so peculiar that
it almost amounts to a separate language. However,
from this part, or properly, from Woody Point south-
wards to Port San Juan, the Aht language is entirely
different.

The latter locality,[1] nearly opposite Cape Flattery,
on the other side of Juan de Fuca Strait, the most
southern part, and the only one on the mainland where
it is spoken, is the special territory of the Pachenahts.
When I knew them, they were, like all of their race, a
dwindling people. A few years earlier, Grant had
estimated them to number a hundred men. In 1863
there were not more than a fifth of that number fit to
manage a canoe, and the total number of the tribe did

[1] "Pachena" of the Indians.

not exceed sixty. War with the Sclallans and Makkahs on the opposite shore, and smallpox, which is more powerful than gunpowder, had so decimated them that, no longer able to hold their own, they had leagued with the Nettinahts, old allies of theirs, for mutual defence. Quixto, the chief, I find described in my notes as a stout fellow, terrible at a bargain, very well disposed towards the whites, as are all his tribe, the husband of four wives, an extraordinary number for the Indians of the coast, and reputed to be rich in blankets and the other gear which constitutes wealth among the aborigines of this part of the British Empire. In their palmy days they had made way as far north as Clayoquat Sound and the Ky-yoh-quaht-cutz in one direction, and with the Tsongersth to the eastward, though that now pusillanimous tribe had generally the best of them. Their eastern border is, however, the Jordan River, but they have a fishing station at the Sombria (Cockles), and several miles up both the Pandora and Jordan Rivers flowing into their bay. Karleit is their western limit.

The Nettinahts [1] are a more powerful tribe; indeed, at the period when the writer of this book was a prisoner in Nootka Sound, they were among the strongest of all the Aht people. Even then, they had four hundred [2] fighting men, and were a people with whom it did not do to be off your guard. They have—or had—many villages, from Pachena Bay [3] to the west and Karleit to the east, besides three villages in Nettinaht Inlet, [4] eleven

---

[1] Or, as they call themselves in their dialect of the Aht, "Dittinahts." Nettinaht is a white man's corruption.

[2] A few years earlier they were estimated at a thousand.

[3] "Klootis" of the Indians.　　　　[4] Known to them as "Etlo."

fishing stations on the Nettinaht River, three stations on the Cowitchan Lake, and one at Sguitz on the Cowitchan River itself, while they sometimes descend as far as Tsanena to plant potatoes. They have thus the widest borders of any Indian tribe in Vancouver Island, and have a high reputation as hunters, whale-fishers, and warriors. Moqulla was then the head chief, but every winter a sub-tribe hunted and fished on the Cowitchan Lake, a sheet of water which I was among the first to visit, and the very first to "lay down" with approximate accuracy. Though nowadays—*Eheu fugaces, Postume, Postume, labuntur anni!*—there is a waggon road to the lake, and, I am told, "a sort of hotel" on the spot where eight-and-twenty years ago we encamped on extremely short rations, though with the soothing knowledge that if only the Fates were kindly and the wind favourable, there were plenty of trout in the water, and a dinner at large in the woods around. In those days most of the Nettinaht villages were fortified with wooden pickets to prevent any night attack, and from its situation, Whyack, the principal one (built on a cliff, stockaded on the seaward side, and reached only by a narrow entrance where the surf breaks continuously), is impregnable to hostile canoemen. This people accordingly carried themselves with a high hand, and bore a name correspondingly bad.

Barclay—or Berkeley Sound—is the home of various petty tribes — Ohyahts, Howchuklisahts, Yu-clul-ahts, Toquahts, Seshahts, and Opechesahts. The two with whom I was best acquainted were the last named. The Seshahts lived at the top of the Alberni Canal

—a long narrow fjord or cleft in the island—and on the Seshaht Islands in the Sound. During the summer months they came for salmon-fishing to Sa ha, or the first rapids on the Kleekort or Saman River,[1] their chief being Ia-pou-noul, who had just succeeded to this office owing to the abdication of his father, though the entire fighting force of the tribe did not number over fifty men. As late as 1859 the Seshahts seized an American ship, the *Swiss Boy*. The Opechesahts, of whom I have very kindly memories, as I encamped with their chief for many days, and explored Sproat Lake in his company, were an offshoot of the Seshahts, and had their home on the Kleekort River, but, owing to a massacre by the now extinct Quallehum (Qualicom) Indians from the opposite coast, who caught them on an island in Sproat Lake, they were reduced to seventeen men, most of them, however, tall, handsome fellows, and good hunters. Chieftainship in that part of the world goes by inheritance. Hence there may be many of these hereditary aristocrats in a very small tribe. Accordingly, few though the Opechesaht warriors were, three men, Quatgenam, Kalooish or Kanash, and Quassoon, a shaggy, thick-set, and tremendously strong individual who crossed the island with me in 1865, were entitled to that rank ; and it may be added that the women of this, the most fresh-water of all the Vancouver tribes, were noted for a more than usual share of good looks.

The Howchuklisahts, whose chief was Maz-o-wennis, numbered forty-five people, including twenty-

[1] They were not permitted this privilege until the whites came to Alberni in August 1860.

eight men. They lived in Ouchucklesit[1] Harbour, off the Alberni Canal; they had also a fishing camp on Henderson Lake, and two or three lodges on the rapid or stream flowing out of that sheet of water, which was discovered and named by me. But they were "bad to deal with."

OHYAHT INDIAN.

The You-clul-ahts of Ucluelt Inlet, ruled by Ia-pou-noul, a wealthy man in blankets and other Indian wealth, numbered about one hundred. The chief of the To-quahts in Pipestem Inlet was Sow-wa-wenes, a middle-aged man, who had an easy task, as his lieges numbered only eleven, so that they were thirty years ago on the eve of extinction. The Ohyahts of Grappler Creek were estimated in 1863 to be about one hundred and seventy-five in fighting strength—which, multiplied by four for women and children, would make them, for that region, an unusu-

[1] Though the orthography of these names is often incorrect, and not even phonetically accurate, I have, in order to avoid the mischief of a confusion of nomenclature, kept to that of the Admiralty Chart.

ally strong community. These figures are probably correct, since the man who made the statement was, after living for years amongst them, eventually murdered by the savages,[1] whom he had trusted too implicitly. Kleesheens, a notorious scoundrel, was their chief. In Clayoquat Sound were the Klahoquahts, Kellsmahts, Ahousahts, Heshquahts, and Mamosahts—the last a little tribe numbering only five men. Indeed, with the exception of the Klahoquahts (who numbered one hundred and sixty men) and the Ahousahts (who claimed two hundred and fifty), these little septs, all devoured by mutual hatred, and frequently at war with each other, were even then dwindling to nothingness. But the Opetsahts, though marked on the Admiralty Chart[2] as a separate tribe, are—or were—only a village of the Ahousahts.

In Nootka Sound, the Muchlahts and Mooachahts lived. In Esperanza Inlet were the villages of two tribes—the Noochahlahts and Ayattisahts, numbering forty and twenty-two men respectively, and chiefed at

---

[1] This was the Banfield who acted as Indian agent in Barclay Sound. He was drowned by Kleetsak, a slave of Kleesheens, capsizing the canoe in which he was sailing, in revenge for a slight passed upon the chief. I went ashore at the Ohyaht village in the same canoe, and was asked whether I was not afraid, "for Banipe was killed in it." There was also a story that the capsize was an accident.

[2] It may be proper to state in this place that the interior details of that chart are, with very few exceptions, from my explorations. But the map on which they were laid down by me has been so often copied by societies, governments, and private individuals without permission (and without acknowledgment), that the author of it has long ceased to claim a property so generally pillaged. The original, however, appeared, with a memoir on the interior—"Das Innere der Vancouver Insel"—which has not yet been translated, in Petermann's *Geographische Mittheilungen*, 1869.

that time by two worthies of the names of Mala-koi-Kennis, and Quak-ate-Komisa, whom we left in the delectable condition of each expecting the other round to cut his and his tribesmen's throats.

North of this inlet were Ky-yoh-quahts, of the Sound of that name (Kaioquat), numbering two hundred and fifty men. To us they were exceedingly friendly, though a trader whom we met had a different tale to tell of their treatment of him. Kanemat, a young man of about twenty-two, was their chief, though the tribe was virtually governed by his mother, a notable lady named Shipally, and at times by his pretty squaw, Wick-anes, and his lively son and heir, Klahe-ek-enes. The Chaykisahts, the Klahosahts, and the Neshahts of Woody Point are the other Aht tribes, though the latter is not included among them by Mr. Sproat. But they speak their language, of which their chief village is its most northern limit.

Everywhere their tribes showed such evident signs of decadence that by this time some of them must be all but extinct. Still, as the whites had not come much in contact with them—though all of them asked us for " lum " (rum), but did not get it, it is clear enough what had been the traders' staple—the " diseases of civilisation " could not be blamed for their decay. Even then the practical extermination of two tribes was so recent that the facts were still fresh in their neighbours' memory. These were the Ekkalahts, who lived at the top of the Alberni Canal, but were all but killed off in the same massacre by which the Opechesahts were decimated. The only survivor was a man named Keekeon, who lived with the Seshahts, most of whom had forgotten even the name of this vanquished little nationality. The other tribe was the Koapinahts (or Koapin-ah), who at that time numbered sixty or seventy people, but at the period to which I refer they were reduced to two adults—a man and a woman—all the rest having been slaughtered a few years earlier by the Kwakiools from the other side of the island, in conjunction with the Neshahts of Woody Point. In after days I learned to know these tribes very familiarly, crossing and recrossing the island with or to them, hunting and canoeing with them, in the woods, up the rivers, or on the lakes, and gathering from their lips

> " This fair report of them who dwell
> In that retirement."

At first sight these "tinkler loons and siclike companie" were by no means attractive. They were frowsy, and, undeniably, they were not clean. But it was only after penetrating their inner ways, after learning the wealth of custom and folk-lore of which they, all unconscious of their riches, were the jealous custodians, that one began to appreciate these primitive folk from a scientific point of view. Even yet, as the writer recalls the days when he was prone to find men more romantic than is possible in "middle life forlorn," it is difficult not to associate the most prosaic of savages with something of the picturesqueness which, in novels at least, used to cling to all their race. For, as the charm of such existence as theirs unfolded itself to the lover of woods and prairies, and lakes and virgin streams, the neglect of soap and of sanitation was forgotten. As Mr. Leland has remarked about the gipsies: " When their lives and legends are known, the ethnologist is apt to think of Tieck's elves, and of the Shang Valley, which was so grim and repulsive from without, but which, once entered, was the gay forecourt of Goblin-land."

In those days little was known—and little cared—about any of the Western tribes, except by the " schooner - men," as the Indians called the roving traders. Their very names were strange to the majority of the Victoria people, and I am told that very few of the colonists of to-day are any better informed. It has therefore been thought fitting that I should go somewhat minutely into the condition of the Indians, at a period when they were more primitive than now, as a slight contribution to the meagre chronicles of a dying race. For if not preserved here, it is likely to perish with almost the last survivor of a little band with whom, during the last two decades, death has been busy.

Among the many inlets which we entered on the cruise Nootka Sound which has enabled me to edit this narrative and its of a less fortunate predecessor, was Nootka memories. Sound. No portion of North-West America was more famous than this spot, for once upon a time it was the former centre of the fur trade, and a locality which more than once figured prominently in diplomatic correspondence. Indeed, so associated was it as the type of this part of the western continent, that in many works the heterogeneous group of savages who inhabit the entire coast between the Columbia River and the end of Vancouver Island was described as the " Nootka-Columbians." More than one species of plant and animal attest the fact of this Sound having been the locality at which the naturalist first broke ground in North-West America. There are, for instance, a *Haliotis Nutkaensis* (an ear shell), a *Rubus Nutkanus* (a raspberry); and a yellow cypress, which, however, attained its chief development on the mainland much farther north, bears among its synonyms that of *Chamæcyparis Nutkaensis*. For though it is undeniable that Ensign Juan Perez discovered it as early as 1779, and named it Port San Lorenzo, after the saint on whose day it was first seen, this fact was unknown or forgotten, when, four years later, Cook entered, and called it King George Sound, though he tells us it was afterwards found that it was called Nootka by the natives. Hence arose the title it has ever since borne, though this was an entire mistake on the great navigator's part, since there is no word in the Aht language at all corresponding to Nootka, unless indeed it is " Nootche," a mountain, which not unlikely Cook mistook for that of the inlet generally. The proofs of the presence of earlier visitors were iron and other tools, familiarity with ships, and two silver spoons of Spanish manufacture, which, we may take it, had been stolen from Perez's ship. The next vessel to enter the Sound was the *Sea Otter*, under the command of Captain James Hanna, who made such a haul in the shape of sea-otter skins that for many years Nootka was the great rendezvous of the fur-traders who cruised as far north as Russian America—now Alaska—and, like Portlock, Dixon, and Meares, charted and named many of the most familiar parts of the British Columbian coast. Meares built the *North-West America* by the aid of Chinese carpenters in Nootka Sound in the winter of 1788–89, this little sloop being the first vessel, except a canoe, ever constructed in the country north of California.

The lucrative trade done by the English and American traders, some of whom, disposing of their furs in China, sailed under the Portuguese flag and fitted out at Macao as the port most readily open to them, determined the Spaniards to assert their rights to the original discovery. This was done by Don Estevan Martinez "taking possession" of the Sound, seizing the vessels there, and erecting a fort to maintain the territory against all comers. A hot diplomatic warfare ensued, the result of which was the Convention of Nootka, by which the Sound was made over to Great Britain; and it was while engaged on this mission of receiving the Sound that Vancouver, conjointly with Quadra, the Spanish commander, discovered that the region it intersects is an island, which for a time bore their joint names, but by general consent has that of Vancouver only attached to it nowadays.

This was in the year 1795. Being now indisputably British territory, Nootka and the coasts north and south of it became more and more frequented by fur-traders, who found, in spite of the increasing scarcity of pelts, and the higher prices which keener competition brought about, an ample profit in buying tolerably cheap on the American coast and selling very dear to the Chinese, whose love for the sea-otter continues unabated. Many of these adventurers were Americans—hailing, for the most part, from Boston. Hence to this day an American is universally known among the North-Western Indians as a " Boston-man," while an Englishman is quite as generally termed a "Kintshautsh man" (King George man), it being during the long reign of George III. that they first became acquainted with our countrymen. Their barter was carried on in knives, copper plates, copper kettles, muskets, brass-hilted swords, soldiers' coats and buttons, pistols, tomahawks, and blankets, which soon superseded the more costly "Kotsaks" of sea-otter until then the principal garment, though the women wore, as they do still at times (or did when I knew the shore), blankets woven out of pine-tree bark. Rum also seemed to have been freely disposed of, and no doubt many of the outrages which early began to mark the intercourse of the brown men and their white visitors were not a little due to this, and to the customs, ever more free than welcome, in which it is the habit of the mariner to indulge when he and the savage forgather. At all events, the natives and their foreign visitors seem to have come very soon into collision. Indeed, it was seldom that a voyage was completed without some outrage on one or both sides, followed by reprisals from the party supposed to have been wronged. Thus part of the crew of the *Imperial Eagle*, under the command of Captain Barclay,[1] who discovered and named in his own honour the Sound so called, were murdered at "Queenhythe,"[2] south of Juan de Fuca Strait, which Barclay was amongst the first to explore, or rather to rediscover. At a later date, namely, in 1805, the *Atahualpa* of Rhode Island was attacked in Millbank

---

[1] Or Berkeley—for the name is spelt both ways.

[2] Destruction Island, in lat. 47° 35'. This was almost the same spot as that in which the Spaniards of Bodega's crew were massacred in 1775, and for this reason they named it Isla de Dolores—the "Island of Sorrows." It is in what is now the State of Washington, U.S.A.

Sound, and her captain, mate, and six seamen were killed.
In 1811 the *Tonquin*, belonging to John Jacob Astor's
romantic fur-trading adventure, which is so well known
from Washington Irving's *Astoria*, was seized by the
savages on this coast, and then blown up by M'Kay, the
chief trader, with the entire crew and their assailants.
The scene of the catastrophe has been stated to be
Nootka, but other commentators have fixed upon Barclay
Sound, and as late as 1863 an intelligent trader informed
me that some ship's timbers, half buried in the sand
there, were attributed by the Indians to some disastrous
event, which he believed to have been the one in question.[1]
I am, however, now inclined to think that in crediting
Nahwitti, at the northern end of Vancouver Island,
with this notable event in the early history of North-
West America,[2] Dr. George Dawson has arrived at the
truth.

To this day—or until very recently—the Indians of
the North-West coast are not accounted very trust-
worthy, and at the period when I knew them they were
suspected of killing several traders and of looting more
than one small vessel, acts which earned for them
frequent visits from the gunboats at Esquimault, and
in several instances the undesirable distinction of

[1] Green Low will even blame Wikananish, who figures in Jewitt's narrative, as the instigator of the outrage.

[2] The Nahwitti Indians. Compare the Tlā-tlī-sī—Kwela and Ne-
kum-ke-lisla septs of the Kwakiool people. They now inhabit a village
named Meloopa, on the south-east side of Hope Island. But their original
hamlet was situated on a small rocky peninsula on the east side of Cape
Commerell, which forms the north point of Vancouver Island. Here
remains of old houses are still to be seen, at a place known to the Indians as
Nahwitti. It was close to this place that the *Tonquin* was blown up.—
Science, vol. ix. p. 341.

INDIAN ENCAMPMENT NEAR THE LANDING-STAGE, ESQUIMAULT.

3

having their villages shelled when they refused to give up the offenders—generally a difficult operation, since it meant pretty well the entire village.

But the most famous of all the piracies of the Western Indians is that of which an account is con-

John Jewitt and the capture of the "Boston" in 1803.

tained in John Jewitt's Narrative. The ostensible author of this work was a Hull blacksmith, the armourer of the *Boston*, an American ship which was seized while lying in Nootka Sound, and the entire crew massacred, with the exception of Jewitt, who was spared owing to his skill as a mechanic being valuable to the Indians, and John Thompson, the sailmaker, who, though left for dead, recovered, and was saved by the tact of Jewitt in representing him to be his father. This happened in March 1803, and from that date until the 20th of July 1805, these two men were kept in slavery to the chief Maquenna or Moqulla, when they were freed by the arrival of the brig *Lydia* of Boston, Samuel Hill master. During this servitude, Jewitt, who seems to have been a man of some education, kept a journal and acquired the Aht language, though the style in which his book is written shows that in preparing it for the press he had obtained the assistance of a more practised writer than himself. Still, his work is a valuable contribution to ethnology. For, omitting the brief but excellent accounts by Cook and Meares, it is the earliest, and, with the exception of Mr. Sproat's lecture, the fullest description of these Indians. It is indeed the only one treating specially on the Nootka people, with whom alone he had any minute acquaintance. Some of the habits he pictures are now obsolete, or greatly modified, but others—it may be said the greater number—are exactly as he notes them to have been eighty-six years ago. Besides the internal evidences of its authenticity, the truth of the adventures described was vouched for at the time by Jewitt's companion in slavery; and though there is no absolute proof of its credibility, it may not be uninteresting to state that, thirty years ago, I conversed with an American sea captain, who, as a boy, distinctly remembered Jewitt working as a blacksmith in the town of Middleton in Connecticut. When the book was first published, in the year 1815, several editions appeared in America, and at least two reprints were called for in England, so that the Narrative enjoyed considerable popularity in the first two decades of the century. Writing in 1840, Robert Green Low, Librarian to the Department of State at Washington, characterises it as "a simple and unpretending narrative, which will, no doubt, in after centuries, be read with interest by the enlightened people of North-West America." Again, in 1845, the same industrious, though not always impartial, historian remarks that "this little book has been frequently reprinted, and, though seldom found in libraries, is much read by boys and seamen in the United States." As copies are now seldom met with, this is no longer the case, though on our cruise in 1863 it was one of the well-thumbed little library of the traders, one of whom had inherited it from William Edy Banfield, whose name has already been mentioned (p. 25). This trader, for many years a well-known man on the out-of-the-way parts of the coast, furnished a curious link between Jewitt's time and our own. For an old Indian told him that he had, as a boy, served in

the family of a chief of Nootka, called Klan-nin-itth, at
the time when Jewitt and Thompson were in slavery;
and that he often assisted Jewitt in making spears,
arrows, and other weapons required for hostile expeditions. He said, further, that the white slave generally
accompanied his owner on visits which he paid to the
Ayhuttisaht, Ahousaht, and Klahoquaht chiefs. This
old man especially remembered Jewitt, who was a
good-humoured fellow, often reciting and singing in
his own language for the amusement of the tribesmen.
He was described as a tall, well-made youth, with a
mirthful countenance, whose dress latterly consisted of
nothing but a mantle of cedar bark. Mr. Sproat, who
obtained his information from the same quarter that
I did, adds that there was a long story of Jewitt's
courting, and finally abducting, the daughter of Waugh-
clagh, the Ahousaht chief. This incident in his career
is not recorded by our author, who, however, was
married to a daughter of Upquesta, an Ayhuttisaht
Indian.

Apart, however, from Jewitt not caring to enlighten
the decent-living puritans of Connecticut too minutely
regarding his youthful escapades, it is not unlikely that
Mr. Banfield's informant mixed up some half-forgotten
legends regarding another white man, who, seventeen
years before Jewitt's captivity, had voluntarily remained
among these Nootka Indians. This was a scapegrace
named John M'Kay,[1] an Irishman, who, after being in
the East India Company's Service in some minor
medical capacity, shipped in 1785 on board the *Captain
Cook* as surgeon's mate, and was left behind in Nootka

[1] "Maccay" (Meares); "M'Key" (Dixon).

Sound, in the hope that he would so ingratiate himself with the natives, as to induce them to refuse furs to any other traders except those with whom he was connected. This man seems to have been an ignorant, untruthful braggart, who contradicted himself in many important particulars. But entire credence may be given to his statement that in a short time he sank into barbarism, becoming as filthy as the dirtiest of his savage companions. For when Captain Hanna saw him in August 1786, the natives had stripped him of his clothes, and obliged him to adopt their dress and habits. He even refused to leave, declaring that he had begun to relish dried fish and whale oil—though, owing to a famine in the Sound, he got little of either—and was well satisfied to stay for another year. After making various excursions in the country about Nootka Sound, during which he came to the conclusion that it was not a part of the American continent, but a chain of detached islands, he gladly deserted his Indian wife, and left with Captain Berkeley in 1787. To " preach, fight, and mend a musket" seems to have been too much for this medical pluralist. His further history I am unable to trace, though, for the sake of historical roundness, it would have been interesting to believe that he was the same M‘Kay who twenty-four years later ended his career so terribly by blowing up the *Tonquin*, with whose son I was well acquainted.

In all of these transactions the head chief of Nootka, or at least of the Mooachahts, figures prominently. This was Maquenna or Moqulla (Jewitt's Maquina), who, with his relative Wikananish, ruled over most of the tribes from here to Nettinaht Inlet. He was a shifty savage, endowed with no small mental ability, and, though at times capable of acts which were almost generous, untrustworthy like most of his race, and when offended ready for any act of vindictiveness. Wikananish was on a visit to Maquenna when the *Discovery* and *Resolution* entered the Sound, and among the relics which Maquenna kept for many years were a brass mortar left by Cook, which in Meares's day was borne before the chief as a portion of his regalia, and three " pieces of a brassy metal formed like cricket bats," on which were the remains of the name and arms of Sir Joseph Banks, and the date 1775—Banks, it may be remembered, being the scientific companion of Cook.   In every subsequent voyage Maquenna figures, and not a few of the outrages committed on that coast were due either to him or to his instigation.   Some, like his attempt to seize Hanna's vessel in 1785, are known from extraneous sources, and others were boasted of by him to Jewitt.   The last of his proceedings of which history has left any record, is the murder of the crew of the *Boston* and the enslavement of Thompson and Jewitt, and in the narrative of the latter we are afforded a final glimpse of this notorious " King." [1]

When I visited Nootka Sound in 1863, fifty-eight Changes since years had passed since the captivity of Jewitt's time. the author of this book.   In the interval

[1] There is a portrait of him, apparently authentic, in Meares's *Voyages*, vol. ii. (1791).   That in the original edition of Jewitt's Narrative, like the plate of the capture of the *Boston*, appears to have been drawn from description, though there is a certain resemblance in it to Meares's sketch made fourteen or fifteen years earlier.   But the scenery, the canoes, the people, and, above all, the palm trees in Nootka Sound, are purely imaginary.

many things had happened. But though the Indians had altered in some respects, they were perhaps less changed than almost any other savages in America since the whites came in contact with them. Eighty-five years had passed since Cook had careened his ships in Resolution Cove, and seventy since Vancouver entered the Sound on his almost more notable voyage. Yet the bricks from the blacksmith's forge, fresh and vitrified as if they had been in contact with the fire only yesterday, were at times dug up from among the rank herbage. The village in Friendly Cove—a spot which not a few mariners found to be very unfriendly—differed in no way from the picture in Cook's *Voyage*; and though some curio-hunting captain had no doubt long ago carried off the mortar and emblazoned brasses, the natives still spoke traditionally of Cook and Vancouver, and were ready to point out the spots where in 1788 Meares built the *North-West America* and the white men had cultivated. Memories of Martinez and Quadra existed in the shape of many legends, of Indians with Iberian features, and of several old people who by tradition (though some of them were old enough to have remembered these navigators), could still repeat the Spanish numerals. And the head chief of the Mooachahts in Friendly Cove—vastly smaller though his tribe was, and much abridged his power—was a grandson of Maquenna, called by the same name, and had many of his worst characteristics. This fact I am likely to remember. For he had been accused of having murdered, in the previous January, Captain Stev of the *Trader*, and since that time no whites had ventured near him. He, however, assured us that the report was simply a scandal raised by the neighbouring tribes, who had long hated him and his people, and would like to see them punished by the arrival of a gunboat, and that in reality the vessel was wrecked, and the white men were drowned. At the same time, among the voices heard that night at the council held in Maquenna's great lodge, supported by the huge beams described by Jewitt, were some in favour of killing his latest visitors, on the principle that dead men tell no tales. But that the Noes had it, the present narrative is the best proof.

So far as their habits were concerned, they were in a condition as primitive as at almost any period since the whites had visited them. Many of the old people were covered only with a mantle of woven pine bark, and beyond a shirt, in most cases made out of a flour sack, a blanket was the sole garment of the majority of the tribesmen. At times when they wanted to receive any goods, they simply pulled off the blanket, wrapped up the articles in it, and went ashore stark naked, with the exception of a piece of skin round the loins. The women wore for the most part no other dress except the blanket and a curious apron made of a fringe of bark strings. All of them painted hideously, the women adding a streak of vermilion down the middle division of the hair, and on high occasions the glittering mica sand, spoken of by Jewitt, was called into requisition. Their customs—and I had plenty of opportunities to study them in the course of the years which followed —were in no way different from what they were in Cook's time. No missionary seemed ever to have visited them, and their religious observances were accordingly still the most unadulterated of paganism. Jewitt's narrative is, however, as might have been expected, very vague on such matters; and, curiously enough, he makes no mention of their characteristic trait of compressing the foreheads of the children, the tribes in Koskeemo Sound squeezing it, while the bones are still cartilaginous, in a conical shape—though the brain is not thereby permanently injured : it is simply displaced.

Since that day, the tribesmen of the west coast of Vancouver Island have grown fewer and fewer. Some of the smaller septs have indeed become extinct, and others must be fast on the wane. They have, however, eaten of the tree of knowledge, and the gunboats have now little occasion to visit them for punitive purposes. Missionaries have even attempted to teach them better manners. The Alberni saw-mills have long been deserted, though other settlers have taken possession of the ground, and several have squatted in Koskeemo Sound, in the hope that the coal-seams there might induce the Pacific steamers to make that remote region their headquarters. Finally, an effort is being made to induce fishermen from the West of Scotland to settle on that coast. There is plenty of work for them, and the Indians nowadays are very little to be feared. Indeed, so far from the successors of Moqulla and Wikananish menacing Donald and Sandy, they will be ready to help them for a consideration; though a great deal of tact and forbearance will be necessary before people so conservative as the hot-tempered Celts work smoothly with a race quite as fiery and quite as wedded to old ways, as the Ahts among whom John Jewitt passed the early years of this century.   R. B.

JOHN JEWITT'S NARRATIVE

—◆—

CHAPTER I

BIRTH, PARENTAGE AND EARLY LIFE OF THE AUTHOR

I WAS born in Boston, a considerable borough town in Lincolnshire, in Great Britain, on the 21st of May, 1783. My father, Edward Jewitt, was by trade a blacksmith, and esteemed among the first in his line of business in that place. At the age of three years I had the misfortune to lose my mother, a most excellent woman, who died in childbed, leaving an infant daughter, who, with myself, and an elder brother by a former marriage of my father, constituted the whole of our family. My father, who considered a good education as the greatest blessing he could bestow on his children, was very particular in paying every attention to us in that respect, always exhorting us to behave well, and endeavouring to impress on our minds the principles of virtue and morality, and no expense in his power was spared to have us instructed in whatever might render us useful and respectable in society. My brother, who was four years older than myself and of a more hardy constitution, he destined for his own trade, but to me he had resolved to give an education superior to that which is to be obtained in a common school, it being his intention that I should adopt one of the learned professions. Accordingly, at the age of twelve he took me from the school in which I had been taught the first rudiments of learning, and placed me under the care of Mr. Moses, a celebrated teacher of an academy at Donnington, about eleven miles from Boston, in order to be instructed in the Latin language, and in some of the higher branches of the mathematics. I there made considerable proficiency in writing, reading, and arithmetic, and obtained a pretty good knowledge of navigation and of surveying; but my progress in Latin was slow, not only owing to the little inclination I felt for learning that language, but to a natural impediment in my speech, which rendered it extremely difficult for me to pronounce it, so that in a short time, with my father's consent, I wholly relinquished the study.

The period of my stay at this place was the most happy of my life. My preceptor, Mr. Moses, was not only a learned, but a virtuous, benevolent, and amiable man, universally beloved by his pupils, who took delight in his instruction, and to whom he allowed every proper amusement that consisted with attention to their studies.

One of the principal pleasures I enjoyed was in attending the fair, which is regularly held twice a year at Donnington, in the spring and in the fall,[1] the second day being wholly devoted to selling horses, a prodigious number of which are brought thither for that purpose.

---

[1] These fairs are still held, though the dates are now May 26th, September 4th, and October 27th.

As the scholars on these occasions were always indulged with a holiday, I cannot express with what eagerness of youthful expectation I used to anticipate these fairs, nor what delight I felt at the various shows, exhibitions of wild beasts, and other entertainments that they presented ; I was frequently visited by my father, who always discovered much joy on seeing me, praised me for my acquirements, and usually left me a small sum for my pocket expenses.

Among the scholars at this academy, there was one named Charles Rice, with whom I formed a particular intimacy, which continued during the whole of my stay. He was my class and room mate, and as the town he came from, Ashby, was more than sixty miles off, instead of returning home, he used frequently during the vacation to go with me to Boston, where he always met with a cordial welcome from my father, who received me on these occasions with the greatest affection, apparently taking much pride in me. My friend in return used to take me with him to an uncle of his in Donnington, a very wealthy man, who, having no children of his own, was very fond of his nephew, and on his account I was always a welcome visitor at the house. I had a good voice, and an ear for music, to which I was always passionately attached, though my father endeavoured to discourage this propensity, considering it (as is too frequently the case) but an introduction to a life of idleness and dissipation ; and, having been remarked for my singing at church, which was regularly attended on Sundays and festival days by the scholars, Mr. Morthrop, my friend Rice's uncle, used frequently to request me to sing ; he was always pleased with my exhibitions of this kind, and it was no doubt one of the means that secured me so gracious a reception at his house. A number of other gentlemen in the place would sometimes send for me to sing at their houses, and as I was not a little vain of my vocal powers, I was much gratified on receiving these invitations, and accepted them with the greatest pleasure.

Thus passed away the two happiest years of my life, when my father, thinking that I had received a sufficient education for the profession he intended me for, took me from school at Donnington in order to apprentice me to Doctor Mason, a surgeon of eminence at Reasby, in the neighbourhood of the celebrated Sir Joseph Banks.[1] With regret did I part from my school acquaintance, particularly my friend Rice, and returned home with my father, on a short visit to my family, preparatory to my intended apprenticeship. The disinclination I ever had felt for the profession my father wished me to pursue, was still further increased on my return. When a child I was always fond of being in the shop, among the workmen, endeavouring to imitate what I saw them do; this disposition so far increased after my leaving the academy, that I could not bear to hear the least mention made of my being apprenticed to a surgeon, and I used so many entreaties with my father to persuade him to give up this plan and learn me his own trade, that he at last consented.

More fortunate would it probably have been for me, had I gratified the wishes of this affectionate parent, in adopting the profession he had chosen for me,

---

[1] The companion of Cook, and for many years President of the Royal Society.

than thus to have induced him to sacrifice them to
mine. However it might have been, I was at length
introduced into the shop, and my natural turn of mind
corresponding with the employment, I became in a short
time uncommonly expert at the work to which I was
set. I now felt myself well contented, pleased with my
occupation, and treated with much affection by my
father, and kindness by my step-mother, my father
having once more entered the state of matrimony, with
a widow much younger than himself, who had been
brought up in a superior manner, and was an amiable
and sensible woman.

About a year after I had commenced this apprenticeship, my father, finding that he could carry on his
business to more advantage in Hull, removed thither
with his family. An event of no little importance to
me, as it in a great measure influenced my future
destiny. Hull being one of the best ports in England,
and a place of great trade, my father had there full
employment for his numerous workmen, particularly in
vessel work. This naturally leading me to an acquaintance with the sailors on board some of the ships: the
many remarkable stories they told me of their voyages
and adventures, and of the manners and customs of the
nations they had seen, excited a strong wish in me to
visit foreign countries, which was increased by my
reading the voyages of Captain Cook, and some other
celebrated navigators.

Thus passed the four years that I lived at Hull, where
my father was esteemed by all who knew him, as a
worthy, industrious, and thriving man. At this period
a circumstance occurred which afforded me the oppor-

tunity I had for some time wished, of gratifying my inclination of going abroad.

Among our principal customers at Hull were the Americans who frequented that port, and from whose conversation my father as well as myself formed the most favourable opinion of that country, as affording an excellent field for the exertions of industry, and a flattering prospect for the establishment of a young man in life. In the summer of the year 1802, during the peace between England and France, the ship *Boston*, belonging to Boston, in Massachusetts, and commanded by Captain John Salter, arrived at Hull, whither she came to take on board a cargo of such goods as were wanted for the trade with the Indians, on the North-West coast of America, from whence, after having taken in a lading of furs and skins, she was to proceed to China, and from thence home to America. The ship having occasion for many repairs and alterations, necessary for so long a voyage, the captain applied to my father to do the smith's work, which was very considerable. That gentleman, who was of a social turn, used often to call at my father's house, where he passed many of his evenings, with his chief and second mates, Mr. B. Delouisa and Mr. William Ingraham,[1] the latter a fine young man of about twenty, of a most amiable temper, and of such affable manners, as gained him the love and attachment of the whole crew. These gentlemen used occasionally to take me with

[1] This William Ingraham must not be confounded with Joseph Ingraham, who also visited Nootka Sound, and played a considerable part in the exploration of the North-West American coast.

them to the theatre, an amusement which I was very fond of, and which my father rather encouraged than objected to, as he thought it a good means of preventing young men, who are naturally inclined to seek for something to amuse them, from frequenting taverns, ale-houses, and places of bad resort, equally destructive of the health and morals, while the stage frequently furnishes excellent lessons of morality and good conduct.

In the evenings that he passed at my father's, Captain Salter, who had for a great number of years been at sea, and seen almost all parts of the world, used sometimes to speak of his voyages, and, observing me listen with much attention to his relations, he one day, when I had brought him some work, said to me in rather a jocose manner, "John, how should you like to go with me?" I answered, that it would give me great pleasure, that I had for a long time wished to visit foreign countries, particularly America, which I had been told so many fine stories of, and that if my father would give his consent, and he was willing to take me with him, I would go.

"I shall be very glad to do it," said he, "if your father can be prevailed on to let you go; and as I want an expert smith for an armourer, the one I have shipped for that purpose not being sufficiently master of his trade, I have no doubt that you will answer my turn well, as I perceive you are both active and ingenious, and on my return to America I shall probably be able to do something much better for you in Boston. I will take the first opportunity of speaking to your father about it, and try to persuade him to consent." He

4

accordingly, the next evening that he called at our house, introduced the subject: my father at first would not listen to the proposal. That best of parents, though anxious for my advantageous establishment in life, could not bear to think of parting with me, but on Captain Salter's telling him of what benefit it would be to me to go the voyage with him, and that it was a pity to keep a promising and ingenious young fellow like myself confined to a small shop in England, when if I had tolerable success I might do so much better in America, where wages were much higher and living cheaper, he at length gave up his objections, and consented that I should ship on board the *Boston* as an armourer, at the rate of thirty dollars per month, with an agreement that the amount due to me, together with a certain sum of money, which my father gave Captain Salter for that purpose, should be laid out by him on the North-West coast in the purchase of furs for my account, to be disposed of in China for such goods as would yield a profit on the return of the ship; my father being solicitous to give me every advantage in his power of well establishing myself in my trade in Boston, or some other maritime town of America. Such were the flattering expectations which this good man indulged respecting me. Alas! the fatal disaster that befell us, not only blasted all these hopes, but involved me in extreme distress and wretchedness for a long period after.

The ship, having undergone a thorough repair and been well coppered, proceeded to take on board her cargo, which consisted of English cloths, Dutch blankets, looking-glasses, beads, knives, razors, etc., which were received from Holland, some sugar and molasses, about twenty hogsheads of rum, including stores for the ship, a great quantity of ammunition, cutlasses, pistols, and three thousand muskets and fowling-pieces. The ship being loaded and ready for sea, as I was preparing for my departure, my father came to me, and, taking me aside, said to me with much emotion, " John, I am now going to part with you, and Heaven only knows if we shall ever again meet. But in whatever part of the world you are, always bear it in mind, that on your own conduct will depend your success in life. Be honest, industrious, frugal, and temperate, and you will not fail, in whatsoever country it may be your lot to be placed, to gain yourself friends. Let the Bible be your guide, and your reliance in any fortune that may befall you, that Almighty Being, who knows how to bring forth good from evil, and who never deserts those who put their trust in Him." He repeated his exhortations to me to lead an honest and Christian life, and to recollect that I had a father, a mother, a brother, and sister, who could not but feel a strong interest in my welfare, enjoining me to write him by the first opportunity that should offer to England, from whatever part of the world I might be in, more particularly on my arrival in Boston. This I promised to do, but long unhappily was it before I was able to fulfil this promise. I then took an affectionate leave of my worthy parent, whose feelings would hardly permit him to speak, and, bidding an affectionate farewell to my brother, sister, and stepmother, who expressed the greatest solicitude for my future fortune, went on board the ship, which proceeded to the Downs, to be ready for the first favourable wind. I found myself well accommodated on board as regarded my work, an iron forge having been erected on deck; this my father had made for the ship on a new plan, for which he afterwards obtained a patent; while a corner of the steerage was appropriated to my vice-bench, so that in bad weather I could work below.

CHAPTER II

VOYAGE TO NOOTKA SOUND

ON the third day of September, 1802, we sailed from the Downs with a fair wind, in company with twenty-four sail of American vessels, most of which were bound home.

I was sea-sick for a few of the first days, but it was of short continuance, and on my recovery I found myself in uncommonly fine health and spirits, and went to work with alacrity at my forge, in putting in order some of the muskets, and making daggers, knives, and small hatchets for the Indian trade, while in wet and stormy weather I was occupied below in filing and polishing them. This was my employment, having but little to do with sailing the vessel, though I used occasionally to lend a hand in assisting the seamen in taking in and making sail.

As I had never before been out of sight of land, I cannot describe my sensations, after I had recovered from the distressing effects of sea-sickness, on viewing the mighty ocean by which I was surrounded, bound only by the sky, while its waves, rising in mountains, seemed every moment to threaten our ruin. Manifest as is the hand of Providence in preserving its creatures from destruction, in no instance is it more so than on the great deep; for whether we consider in its tumultuary motions the watery deluge that each moment menaces to overwhelm us, the immense violence of its shocks, the little that interposes between us and death, a single plank forming our only security, which, should it unfortunately be loosened, would plunge us at once into the abyss, our gratitude ought strongly to be excited towards that superintending Deity who in so wonderful a manner sustains our lives amid the waves.

We had a pleasant and favourable passage of twenty-nine days to the Island of St. Catherine,[1] on the coast of Brazils, where the captain had determined to stop for a few days to wood and water. This place belongs to the Portuguese. On entering the harbour, we were saluted by the fort, which we returned. The next day the governor of the island came on board of us with his suite; Captain Salter received him with much respect, and invited him to dine with him, which he accepted. The ship remained at St. Catherine's four days, during which time we were busily employed in taking in wood, water, and fresh provisions, Captain Salter thinking it best to furnish himself here with a full supply for his voyage to the North-West coast, so as not to be obliged to stop at the Sandwich Islands. St. Catherine's is a very commodious place for vessels to stop at that are bound round Cape Horn, as it abounds with springs of fine water, with excellent oranges, plantains, and bananas.

Having completed our stores, we put to sea, and on the twenty-fifth of December, at length passed Cape

[1] Santa Catharina.

Horn, which we had made no less than thirty-six days before, but were repeatedly forced back by contrary winds, experiencing very rough and tempestuous weather in doubling it.

Immediately after passing Cape Horn, all our dangers and difficulties seemed to be at an end; the weather became fine, and so little labour was necessary on board the ship, that the men soon recovered from their fatigue and were in excellent spirits. A few days after we fell in with an English South Sea whaling ship homeward bound,[1] which was the only vessel we spoke with on our voyage. We now took the trade wind or monsoon, during which we enjoyed the finest weather possible, so that for the space of a fortnight we were not obliged to reeve a topsail or to make a tack, and so light was the duty and easy the life of the sailors during this time, that they appeared the happiest of any people in the world.

Captain Salter, who had been for many years in the East India trade, was a most excellent seaman, and preserved the strictest order and discipline on board his ship, though he was a man of mild temper and conciliating manners, and disposed to allow every indulgence to his men, not inconsistent with their duty. We had on board a fine band of music, with which on Saturday nights, when the weather was pleasant, we were accustomed to be regaled, the captain ordering them to play for several hours for the amusement of the crew. This to me was most delightful, especially during the serene evenings we experienced in traversing the

---

[1] This is now, so far as Great Britain is concerned, a reminiscence of a vanished trade: the South Sea whaling is extinct.

Southern Ocean. As for myself, during the day I was constantly occupied at my forge, in refitting or repairing some of the ironwork of the vessel, but principally in making tomahawks, daggers, etc., for the North-West coast.

During the first part of our voyage we saw scarcely any fish, excepting some whales, a few sharks, and flying fish; but after weathering Cape Horn we met with numerous shoals of sea porpoises, several of whom we caught, and as we had been for some time without fresh provisions, I found it not only a palatable, but really a very excellent food. To one who has never before seen them, a shoal of these fish [1] presents a very striking and singular appearance; beheld at a distance coming towards a vessel, they look not unlike a great number of small black waves rolling over one another in a confused manner, and approaching with great swiftness. As soon as a shoal is seen, all is bustle and activity on board the ship, the grains and the harpoons are immediately got ready, and those who are best skilled in throwing them take their stand at the bow and along the gunwale, anxiously awaiting the welcome troop as they come, gambolling and blowing around the vessel, in search of food. When pierced with the harpoon and drawn on board, unless the fish is instantly killed by the stroke, which rarely happens, it utters most pitiful cries, greatly resembling those of an infant. The flesh, cut into steaks and broiled, is not unlike very coarse beef, and the harslet in appearance and taste is so much like that of a hog,

[1] The zoological reader does not require to be told that the porpoise, a very general term applied by sailors to many small species of cetaceans, is not a " fish."

that it would be no easy matter to distinguish the one from the other; from this circumstance the sailors have given the name of the herring hog[1] to this fish. I was told by some of the crew, that if one of them happens to free itself from the grains or harpoons, when struck, all the others, attracted by the blood, immediately quit the ship and give chase to the wounded one, and as soon as they overtake it, immediately tear it in pieces. We also caught a large shark, which had followed the ship for several days, with a hook which I made for the purpose, and although the flesh was by no means equal to that of the herring hog, yet to those destitute as we were of anything fresh, I found it eat very well. After passing the Cape, when the sea had become calm, we saw great numbers of albatrosses, a large brown and white bird of the goose kind, one of which Captain Salter shot, whose wings measured from their extremities fifteen feet. One thing, however, I must not omit mentioning, as it struck me in a most singular and extraordinary manner. This was, that on passing Cape Horn in December, which was midsummer in that climate, the nights were so light, without any moon, that we found no difficulty whatever in reading small print, which we frequently did during our watches.

[1] *Porc poisson* of the French, of which porpoise is simply a corruption.

CHAPTER III

INTERCOURSE WITH THE NATIVES — MAQUINA —
SEIZURE OF THE VESSEL AND MURDER OF THE
CREW

IN this manner, with a fair wind and easy weather from
the 28th of December, the period of our passing Cape
Horn, we pursued our voyage to the northward until
the 12th of March, 1803, when we made Woody Point
in Nootka Sound, on the North-West coast of America.
We immediately stood up the Sound for Nootka, where [1]
Captain Salter had determined to stop, in order to supply
the ship with wood and water before proceeding up the
coast to trade. But in order to avoid the risk of any
molestation or interruption to his men from the Indians
while thus employed, he proceeded with the ship about
five miles to the northward of the village, which is
situated on Friendly Cove, and sent out his chief mate
with several of the crew in the boat to find a good
place for anchoring her. After sounding for some time,
they returned with information that they had discovered
a secure place for anchorage, on the western side of an
inlet or small bay, at about half a mile from the coast,

[1] By "Nootka," Friendly Cove, or ' Yucuaht," is meant ; there is no
special place of that name ; the word, indeed, is unknown to the natives.
Woody Point, or Cape Cook, is in lat. 50° 6' 31" N.

near a small island which protected it from the sea, and where there was plenty of wood and excellent water. The ship accordingly came to anchor in this place, at twelve o'clock at night, in twelve fathom water, muddy bottom, and so near the shore that to prevent the ship from winding we secured her by a hawser to the trees.

On the morning of the next day, the 13th, several of the natives came on board in a canoe from the village of Nootka, with their king, called Maquina, who appeared much pleased on seeing us, and with great seeming cordiality welcomed Captain Salter and his officers to his country. As I had never before beheld a savage of any nation, it may readily be supposed that the novelty of their appearance, so different from any people that I had hitherto seen, excited in me strong feelings of surprise and curiosity. I was, however, particularly struck with the looks of their king, who was a man of a dignified aspect, about six feet in height and extremely straight and well proportioned; his features were in general good, and his face was rendered remarkable by a large Roman nose, a very uncommon form of feature among these people; his complexion was of a dark copper hue, though his face, legs, and arms were, on this occasion, so covered with red paint, that their natural colour could scarcely be perceived; his eyebrows were painted black in two broad stripes like a new moon, and his long black hair, which shone with oil, was fastened in a bunch on the top of his head and strewed or powdered all over with white down, which gave him a most curious and extraordinary appearance. He was dressed in a large mantle or cloak of the black sea-otter skin, which reached to his knees, and was fastened around his middle by a broad belt of the cloth of the country, wrought or painted with figures of several colours; this dress was by no means unbecoming, but, on the contrary, had an air of savage magnificence. His men were habited in mantles of the same cloth, which is made from the bark of a tree,[1] and has some resemblance to straw matting; these are nearly square, and have two holes in the upper part large enough to admit the arms; they reach as low as the knees, and are fastened round their bodies with a belt about four inches broad of the same cloth.

From his having frequently visited the English and American ships that traded to the coast, Maquina had learned the signification of a number of English words, and in general could make himself pretty well understood by us in our own language. He was always the first to go on board such ships as came to Nootka, which he was much pleased in visiting, even when he had no trade to offer, as he always received some small present, and was in general extremely well treated by the commanders. He remained on board of us for some time, during which the captain took him into the cabin and treated him with a glass of rum—these people being very fond of distilled spirits—and some biscuit and molasses, which they prefer to any kind of food that we can offer them.[2]

[1] The white pine (*Pinus monticola*). This is employed for making blankets trimmed with sea-otter fur, but the mats used in their canoes are made of cedar bark (*Thuja gigantea*).

[2] This is still true. Many years ago, when there was a threat of Indian trouble at Victoria, Sir James Douglas, famous as the first governor of British Columbia, and still more celebrated as a factor of the Hudson Bay Company, immediately allayed the rising storm by ordering a keg of treacle and a box of biscuit to be opened. Instantly the knives and muskets were tossed aside, and the irate savages fell to these homely dainties with

As there are seldom many furs to be purchased at this place, and it was not fully the season, Captain Salter had put in here not so much with an expectation of trading, as to procure an ample stock of wood and water for the supply of the ship on the coast, thinking it more prudent to take it on board at Nootka, from the generally friendly disposition of the people, than to endanger the safety of his men in sending them on shore for that purpose among the more ferocious natives of the north.

With this view, we immediately set about getting our water-casks in readiness, and the next and two succeeding days, part of the crew were sent on shore to cut pine timber, and assist the carpenter in making it into yards and spars for the ship, while those on board were employed in refitting the rigging, repairing the sails, etc., when we proceeded to take in our wood and water as expeditiously as possible, during which time I kept myself busily employed in repairing the muskets, making knives, tomaxes,[1] etc., and doing such ironwork as was wanted for the ship.

Meantime more or less of the natives came on board of us daily, bringing with them fresh salmon, with which they supplied us in great plenty, receiving in return some trifling articles. Captain Salter was always very particular, before admitting these people on board, to see that they had no arms about them, by obliging them

the best of goodwill to all concerned. "Dear me! dear me! there is nothing like a little molasses," was the sage governor's remark. At the Alberni sawmills, on the West coast, the invariable midday meal of the Indians loading lumber was coarse ship's biscuit dipped in a tin basin of the cheapest treacle, around which the mollified tribesmen squatted.

[1] Tomahawks (little hatchets) in more familiar language.

indiscriminately to throw off their garments, so that he felt perfectly secure from any attack.

On the 15th the king came on board with several of his chiefs; he was dressed as before in his magnificent otter-skin robe, having his face highly painted, and his hair tossed with the white down, which looked like snow. His chiefs were dressed in mantles of the country cloth of its natural colour, which is a pale yellow; these were ornamented with a broad border, painted or wrought in figures of several colours, representing men's heads, various animals, etc., and secured around them by a belt like that of the king, from which it was distinguished only by being narrower: the dress of the common people is of the same fashion, and differs from that of the chiefs in being of a coarser texture, and painted red, of one uniform colour.

Captain Salter invited Maquina and his chiefs to dine with him, and it was curious to see how these people (when they eat) seat themselves (in their country fashion, upon our chairs) with their feet under them crossed like Turks. They cannot endure the taste of salt, and the only thing they would eat with us was the ship bread, which they were very fond of, especially when dipped in molasses; they had also a great liking for tea and coffee when well sweetened. As iron weapons and tools of almost every kind are in much request among them, whenever they came on board they were always very attentive to me, crowding around me at the forge, as if to see in what manner I did my work, and in this way became quite familiar, a circumstance, as will be seen in the end, of great importance to me. The salmon which they brought us furnished a most delicious treat to men who for a long time had lived wholly on salt provisions, excepting such few sea fish as we had the good fortune occasionally to take. We indeed feasted most luxuriously, and flattered ourselves that we should not want while on the coast for plenty of fresh provisions, little imagining the fate that awaited us, and that this dainty food was to prove the unfortunate lure to our destruction!

On the 19th the king came again on board, and was invited by the captain to dine with him. He had much conversation with Captain Salter, and informed him that there were plenty of wild ducks and geese near Friendly Cove, on which the captain made him a present of a double-barrelled fowling - piece, with which he appeared to be greatly pleased, and soon after went on shore.

On the 20th we were nearly ready for our departure, having taken in what wood and water we were in want of.

The next day Maquina came on board with nine pair of wild ducks, as a present; at the same time he brought with him the gun, one of the locks of which he had broken, telling the captain that it was *peshak*,[1] that is, bad. Captain Salter was very much offended at this observation, and, considering it as a mark of contempt for his present, he called the king a liar, adding other opprobrious terms, and, taking the gun from him, tossed it indignantly into the cabin, and, calling me to him, said, "John, this fellow has broken this beautiful fowling-piece, see if you can mend it." On examining it, I told

---

[1] *Pesh-shuak, Wikoo,* or *Chuuk* is also used in the same sense, but the first word is most frequently employed.

him that it could be done. As I have already observed, Maquina knew a number of English words, and unfortunately understood but too well the meaning of the reproachful terms that the captain addressed to him. He said not a word in reply, but his countenance sufficiently expressed the rage he felt, though he exerted himself to suppress it, and I observed him, while the captain was speaking, repeatedly put his hand to his throat, and rub it upon his bosom, which he afterwards told me was to keep down his heart, which was rising into his throat and choking him. He soon after went on shore with his men, evidently much discomposed.

On the morning of the 22nd the natives came off to us as usual with salmon, and remained on board; when about noon Maquina came alongside, with a considerable number of his chiefs and men in their canoes, who, after going through the customary examination, were admitted into the ship. He had a whistle in his hand, and over his face a very ugly mask of wood, representing the head of some wild beast, appeared to be remarkably good-humoured and gay, and whilst his people sang and capered about the deck, entertaining us with a variety of antic trick and gestures, he blew his whistle to a kind of tune which seemed to regulate their motions. As Captain Salter was walking on the quarter-deck, amusing himself with their dancing, the king came up to him and inquired when he intended to go to sea? He answered, "To-morrow." Maquina then said, "You love salmon—much in Friendly Cove, why not go there and catch some?" The captain thought that it would be very desirable to have a good supply of these fish for the voyage, and, on consulting with Mr. Delouisa, it was agreed to send part of the crew on shore after dinner with the seine, in order to procure a quantity. Maquina and his chiefs stayed and dined on board, and after dinner the chief mate went off with nine men in the jolly-boat and yawl, to fish at Friendly Cove, having set the steward on shore at our watering place, to wash the captain's clothes.

Shortly after the departure of the boats, I went down to my vice-bench in the steerage, where I was employed in cleaning muskets. I had not been there more than an hour, when I heard the men hoisting in the longboat, which, in a few minutes after, was succeeded by a great bustle and confusion on deck. I immediately ran up the steerage stairs, but scarcely was my head above deck, when I was caught by the hair by one of the savages, and lifted from my feet; fortunately for me, my hair being short, and the ribbon with which it was tied slipping, I fell from his hold into the steerage. As I was falling he struck at me with an axe, which cut a deep gash in my forehead, and penetrated the skull, but in consequence of his losing his hold I luckily escaped the full force of the blow, which otherwise would have cleft my head in two. I fell, stunned and senseless, upon the floor; how long I continued in this situation I know not, but on recovering my senses, the first thing that I did was to try to get up, but so weak was I, from the loss of blood, that I fainted and fell. I was, however, soon recalled to my recollection by three loud shouts or yells from the savages, which convinced me that they had got possession of the ship. It is impossible for me to describe my feelings at this terrific

5

sound. Some faint idea may be formed of them by those who have known what it is to half waken from a hideous dream and still think it real. Never, no, never shall I lose from my mind the impression of that dreadful moment. I expected every instant to share the wretched fate of my unfortunate companions, and when I heard the song of triumph, by which these infernal yells was succeeded, my blood ran cold in my veins.

Having at length sufficiently recovered my senses to look around me, after wiping the blood from my eyes, I saw that the hatch of the steerage was shut. This was done, as I afterwards discovered, by order of Maquina, who, on seeing the savage strike at me with the axe, told him not to hurt me, for that I was the armourer, and would be useful to them in repairing their arms; while at the same time, to prevent any of his men from injuring me, he had the hatch closed. But to me this circumstance wore a very different appearance, for I thought that these barbarians had only prolonged my life in order to deprive me of it by the most cruel tortures.

I remained in this horrid state of suspense for a very long time, when at length the hatch was opened, and Maquina, calling me by name, ordered me to come up. I groped my way up as well as I was able, being almost blinded with the blood that flowed from my wound, and so weak as with difficulty to walk. The king, on perceiving my situation, ordered one of his men to bring a pot of water to wash the blood from my face, which having done, I was able to see distinctly with one of my eyes, but the other was so swollen from my wound, that it was closed. But what a terrific spectacle met my eyes: six naked savages, standing in a circle around me, covered with the blood of my murdered comrades, with their daggers uplifted in their hands, prepared to strike. I now thought my last moment had come, and recommended my soul to my Maker.

The king, who, as I have already observed, knew enough of English to make himself understood, entered the circle, and, placing himself before me, addressed me nearly in the following words: "John—I speak—you no say no; You say no—daggers come!" He then asked me if I would be his slave during my life—if I would fight for him in his battles, if I would repair his muskets and make daggers and knives for him —with several other questions, to all of which I was careful to answer, yes. He then told me that he would spare my life, and ordered me to kiss his hands and feet to show my submission to him, which I did. In the meantime his people were very clamorous to have me put to death, so that there should be none of us left to tell our story to our countrymen, and prevent them from coming to trade with them ; but the king in the most determined manner opposed their wishes, and to his favour am I wholly indebted for my being yet among the living.

As I was busy at work at the time of the attack, I was without my coat, and what with the coldness of the weather, my feebleness from loss of blood, the pain of my wound, and the extreme agitation and terror that I still felt, I shook like a leaf, which the king observing, went into the cabin, and, bringing up a greatcoat that belonged to the captain, threw it over my shoulders, telling me to drink some rum from a bottle which he handed me, at the same time giving me to understand that it would be good for me, and keep me from trembling as I did. I took a draught of it, after which, taking me by the hand, he led me to the quarter-deck, where the most horrid sight presented itself that ever my eyes witnessed. The heads of our unfortunate captain and his crew, to the number of twenty-five, were all arranged in a line,[1] and Maquina, ordering one of his people to bring a head, asked me whose it was: I answered, the captain's. In like manner the others were showed me, and I told him the names, excepting a few that were so horribly mangled that I was not able to recognise them.

I now discovered that all our unfortunate crew had been massacred, and learned that, after getting possession of the ship, the savages had broke open the arm-chest and magazine, and, supplying themselves with ammunition and arms, sent a party on shore to attack our men, who had gone thither to fish, and, being joined by numbers from the village, without difficulty overpowered and murdered them, and, cutting off their heads, brought them on board, after throwing their bodies into the sea. On looking upon the deck, I saw it entirely covered with the blood of my poor comrades, whose throats had been cut with their own jack-knives, the savages having seized the opportunity, while they were busy in hoisting in the boat, to grapple with them, and overpower them by their numbers ; in the scuffle the captain was thrown

---

[1] The Indians of the North-West coast and the wooded region protected by the great rivers always take heads as trophies. The heads are subsequently fixed on poles in front of their cedar-board lodges. The prairie Indians and the tribes east of the Rocky Mountains generally take, and always took, scalps alone, owing, perhaps, to the difficulty of carrying heads. This is no obstacle to fighting men travelling in canoes, on the bows of which they are often fastened while the warriors are returning from hostile expeditions.

overboard, and despatched by those in the canoes, who immediately cut off his head. What I felt on this occasion, may be more readily conceived than expressed.

After I had answered his questions, Maquina took my silk handkerchief from my neck and bound it around my head, placing over the wound a leaf of tobacco, of which we had a quantity on board. This was done at my desire, as I had often found, from personal experience, the benefit of this application to cuts.

Maquina then ordered me to get the ship under weigh for Friendly Cove. This I did by cutting the cables, and sending some of the natives aloft to loose the sails, which they performed in a very bungling manner. But they succeeded so far in loosing the jib and top-sails, that, with the advantage of fair wind, I succeeded in getting the ship into the Cove, where, by order of the king, I ran her ashore on a sandy beach, at eight o'clock at night.

CHAPTER IV

RECEPTION OF JEWITT BY THE SAVAGES — ESCAPE OF THOMPSON—ARRIVAL OF NEIGHBOURING TRIBES —AN INDIAN FEAST.

WE were received by the inhabitants of the village, men, women, and children, with loud shouts of joy, and a most horrible drumming with sticks upon the roofs and sides of their houses,[1] in which they had also stuck a great number of lighted pine torches, to welcome their king's return, and congratulate him on the success of his enterprise.

Maquina then took me on shore to his house, which was very large, and filled with people—where I was received with much kindness by the women, particularly those belonging to the king, who had no less than nine wives, all of whom came around me, expressing much sympathy for my misfortune, gently stroking and patting my head in an encouraging and soothing manner, with words expressive of condolence. How sweet is compassion even from savages! Those who have been in a similar situation, can alone truly appreciate its value.

[1] A common mode of expressing joy. During dancing and singing this goes on continually.

In the meantime all the warriors of the tribe, to the number of five hundred,[1] had assembled at the king's house, to rejoice for their success. They exulted greatly in having taken our ship, and each one boasted of his own particular exploits in killing our men, but they were in general much dissatisfied with my having been suffered to live, and were very urgent with Maquina to deliver me to them, to be put to death, which he obstinately refused to do, telling them that he had promised me my life, and would not break his word; and that, besides, I knew how to repair and to make arms, and should be of great use to them.

The king then seated me by him, and ordered his women to bring him something to eat, when they set before him some dried clams and train-oil, of which he ate very heartily, and encouraged me to follow his example, telling me to eat much, and take a great deal of oil, which would make me strong and fat. Notwithstanding his praise of this new kind of food, I felt no disposition to indulge in it, both the smell and taste being loathsome to me; and had it been otherwise, such was the pain I endured, the agitation of my mind, and the gloominess of my reflections, that I should have felt very little inclination for eating.

Not satisfied with his first refusal to deliver me up to them, the people again became clamorous that Maquina should consent to my being killed, saying that not one of us ought to be left alive to give information to others of our countrymen, and prevent them from coming to

[1] In 1863, when I made a special inquiry, the whole number of adult males in the Mooachaht tribe (the so-called Nootkans) was one hundred and fifty.

trade, or induce them to revenge the destruction of our ship, and they at length became so boisterous, that he caught up a large club in a passion, and drove them all out of the house. During this scene, a son of the king, about eleven years old, attracted no doubt by the singularity of my appearance, came up to me: I caressed him; he returned my attentions with much apparent pleasure, and considering this as a fortunate opportunity to gain the good will of the father, I took the child on my knee, and, cutting the metal buttons from off the coat I had on, I tied them around his neck. At this he was highly delighted, and became so much attached to me, that he would not quit me.

The king appeared much pleased with my attention to his son, and, telling me that it was time to go to sleep, directed me to lie with his son next to him, as he was afraid lest some of his people would come while he was asleep and kill me with their daggers. I lay down as he ordered me, but neither the state of my mind nor the pain I felt would allow me to sleep.

About midnight I was greatly alarmed by the approach of one of the natives, who came to give information to the king that there was one of the white men alive, who had knocked him down as he went on board the ship at night. This Maquina communicated to me, giving me to understand that as soon as the sun rose he should kill him. I endeavoured to persuade him to spare his life, but he bade me be silent and go to sleep. I said nothing more, but lay revolving in my mind what method I could devise to save the life of this man. What a consolation, thought I, what a happiness would it prove to me in my forlorn state among these heathens, to have a Christian and one of my own countrymen for a companion, and how greatly would it alleviate and lighten the burden of my slavery.

As I was thinking of some plan for his preservation, it all at once came into my mind that this man was probably the sail-maker of the ship, named Thompson, as I had not seen his head among those on deck, and knew that he was below at work upon sails not long before the attack. The more I thought of it, the more probable it appeared to me, and as Thompson was a man nearly forty years of age, and had an old look, I conceived it would be easy to make him pass for my father, and by this means prevail on Maquina to spare his life. Towards morning I fell into a dose, but was awakened with the first beams of the sun by the king, who told me he was going to kill the man who was on board the ship, and ordered me to accompany him. I rose and followed him, leading with me the young prince, his son.

On coming to the beach, I found all the men of the tribe assembled. The king addressed them, saying that one of the white men had been found alive on board the ship, and requested their opinion as to saving his life or putting him to death. They were unanimously for the latter. This determination he made known to me. Having arranged my plan, I asked him, pointing to the boy, whom I still held by the hand, if he loved his son. He answered that he did. I then asked the child if he loved his father, and on his replying in the affirmative, I said, "And I also love mine." I then threw myself on my knees at Maquina's feet, and implored him, with tears in my eyes, to spare my father's life, if the man on board should prove to be him, telling him that if he killed my father, it was my wish that he should kill me too, and that if he did not, I would kill myself—and that he would thus lose my services; whereas, by sparing my father's life, he would preserve mine, which would be of great advantage 'to him, by my repairing and making arms for him.

Maquina appeared moved by my entreaties, and promised not to put the man to death if he should be my father. He then explained to his people what I had said, and ordered me to go on board and tell the man to come on shore. To my unspeakable joy, on going into the hold, I found that my conjecture was true. Thompson was there. He had escaped without any injury, excepting a slight wound in the nose, given him by one of the savages with a knife, as he attempted to come on deck, during the scuffle. Finding the savages in possession of the ship, as he afterwards informed me, he secreted himself in the hold, hoping for some chance to make his escape; but that, the Indian who came on board in the night approaching the place where he was, he supposed himself discovered, and, being determined to sell his life as dearly as possible, as soon as he came within his reach, he knocked him down, but the Indian, immediately springing up, ran off at full speed.

I informed him, in a few words, that all our men had been killed; that the king had preserved my life, and had consented to spare his on the supposition that he was my father, an opinion which he must be careful not to undeceive them in, as it was his only safety. After giving him his cue, I went on shore with him, and presented him to Maquina, who immediately knew him to be the sail-maker, and was much pleased, observing that he could make sails for his canoe. He then took us to his house, and ordered something for us to eat.

On the 24th and 25th, the natives were busily employed in taking the cargo out of the ship, stripping her of her sails and rigging, cutting away the spars and masts, and, in short, rendering her as complete a wreck as possible, the muskets, ammunition, cloth, and all the principal articles taken from her, being deposited in the king's house.

While they were thus occupied, each one taking what he liked, my companion and myself being obliged to aid them, I thought it best to secure the accounts and papers of the ship, in hopes that on some future day I might have it in my power to restore them to the owners. With this view I took possession of the captain's writing-desk, which contained the most of them, together with some paper and implements for writing. I had also the good fortune to find a blank account-book, in which I resolved, should it be permitted me, to write an account of our capture, and the most remarkable occurrences that I should meet with during my stay among these people, fondly indulging the hope that it would not be long before some vessel would arrive to release us. I likewise found in the cabin a small volume of sermons, a Bible, and a Common Prayer-book of the Church of England, which furnished me and my comrade great consolation in the midst of our mournful servitude, and enabled me, under the favour of Divine Providence, to support with firmness the miseries of a life which I might otherwise have found beyond my strength to endure.

As these people set no value upon things of this kind, I found no difficulty in appropriating them to myself, by putting them in my chest, which, though it had been broken open and rifled by the savages, as I still had the key, I without much difficulty secured. In this I also put some small tools belonging to the ship, with several other articles, particularly a journal kept by the second mate, Mr. Ingraham, and a collection of drawings and views of places taken by him, which I had the good fortune to preserve, and on my arrival at Boston, I gave them to a connection of his, the Honourable Judge Dawes, who sent them to his family in New York.

On the 26th, two ships were seen standing in for Friendly Cove. At their first appearance the inhabitants were thrown into great confusion, but, soon collecting a number of muskets and blunderbusses, ran to the shore, from whence they kept up so brisk a fire at them, that they were evidently afraid to approach nearer, and, after firing a few rounds of grape-shot, which did no harm to any one, they wore ship and stood out to sea. These ships, as I afterwards learned, were the *Mary* and *Juno* of Boston.

They were scarcely out of sight when Maquina expressed much regret that he had permitted his people to fire at them, being apprehensive that they would give information to others in what manner they had been received, and prevent them from coming to trade with him.

A few days after hearing of the capture of the ship,

there arrived at Nootka a great number of canoes filled
with savages from no less than twenty tribes to the
north and south. Among those from the north were
the Ai-tiz-zarts,[1] Schoo-mad-its,[2] Neu-wit-ties,[3] Savin-
nars,[4] Ah-owz-arts,[5] Mo-watch-its,[6] Suth-setts,[7] Neu-
chad-lits,[8] Mich-la-its,[9] and Cay-u-quets,[10] the most of
whom were considered as tributary to Nootka. From
the south, the Aytch-arts [11] and Esqui-ates,[12] also tributary, with the Kla-oo-quates,[13] and the Wickannish, a
large and powerful tribe about two hundred miles
distant.

These last were better clad than most of the others,
and their canoes wrought with much greater skill;

[1] Ayhuttisahts.

[2] This name is unknown to me.

[3] Nahwittis, or Flatlashekwill, an almost vanished tribe, join the north
end of Vancouver Island (Goletas Channel, Galliano Island, and west-
ward to Cape Scott).

[4] The name of some village, not a tribe.

[5] Ahousahts.

[6] Mooachahts. The "Nootkans" proper of Friendly Cove.

[7] Seshahts, but they are to the south (Alberni Canal) and Barclay
Sound.

[8] Noochahlahts (lat. 49° 47′ 20″ N.).

[9] Muchlahts, or Quaquina arm.

[10] Ky-yoh-quahts.

[11] This is probably another spelling of the E-cha-chahts.

[12] Hishquayahts (lat. 49° 27′ 31″ N., long. 126° 25′ 27″ W.

[13] Klahoquahts. This and the other tribes mentioned in the text are no
longer tributary to the Mooachahts, and there is no "Wickannish" tribe.
As we have already seen (p. 38), it is the name of an individual—probably
the chief of the Klahoquahts. It is a common name. The Nettinahts
and the Klahoquahts are still renowned in canoe-making. They chisel
them out of the great cedar (*Thuja gigantea*) trees in this district, for
sale to other tribes. But Jewitt, who had no personal knowledge of the
homes of these tribes, makes sad havoc of their names and the direction
from which they came.

they are furnished with sails as well as paddles, and, with the advantage of a fair breeze, are usually but twenty-four hours on their passage.

Maquina, who was very proud of his new acquisition, was desirous of welcoming these visitors in the European manner. He accordingly ordered his men, as the canoes approached, to assemble on the beach with loaded muskets and blunderbusses, placing Thompson at the cannon, which had been brought from the ship and laid upon two long sticks of timber in front of the village ; then, taking a speaking trumpet in his hand, he ascended with me the roof of his house, and began drumming or beating upon the boards with a stick most violently.

Nothing could be more ludicrous than the appearance of this motley group of savages collected on the shore, dressed as they were with their ill-gotten finery in the most fantastic manner, some in women's smocks, taken from our cargo, others in *Kotsacks*,[1] (or cloaks) of blue, red, or yellow broadcloth, with stockings drawn over their heads, and their necks hung round with numbers of powder-horns, shot-bags, and cartouch-boxes, some of them having no less than ten muskets apiece on their shoulders, and five or six daggers in their girdles. Diverting indeed was it to see them all squatted upon the beach, holding their muskets perpendicularly with

---

[1] *Kootsik*, the "cotsack" of Meares. *Kootsik-poom* is the pin by which the Indian blanket cloak is fastened. In Meares's time the people dressed in kootsiks of sea-otter skin. But even then they were getting so fond of blankets, that without "woollens" among the barter, trade was difficult. In fifteen years they learned a better use for sea-otters worth £20 apiece than to make cloaks of them.

the butt pressed upon the sand, instead of against their shoulders, and in this position awaiting the order to fire.

Maquina, at last, called to them with his trumpet to fire, which they did in the most awkward and timid manner, with their muskets hard pressed upon the ground as above-mentioned. At the same moment the cannon was fired by Thompson, immediately on which they threw themselves back and began to roll and tumble over the sand as if they had been shot, when, suddenly springing up, they began a song of triumph, and, running backward and forward upon the shore, with the wildest gesticulations, boasted of their exploits, and exhibited as trophies what they had taken from us. Notwithstanding the unpleasantness of my situation, and the feelings that this display of our spoils excited, I could not avoid laughing at the strange appearance of these savages, their awkward movements, and the singular contrast of their dress and arms.

When the ceremony was concluded, Maquina invited the strangers to a feast at his house, consisting of whale-blubber, smoked herring spawn, and dried fish and train-oil, of which they ate most plentifully. The feast being over, the trays out of which they ate, and other things, were immediately removed to make room for the dance, which was to close the entertainment. This was performed by Maquina's son, the young prince Sat-sat-sok-sis, whom I have already spoken of, in the following manner :—

Three of the principal chiefs, drest in their otter-skin mantles, which they wear only on extraordinary occasions and at festivals, having their heads covered over with white down and their faces highly painted, came forward into the middle of the room, each furnished with a bag filled with white down, which they scattered around in such a manner as to represent a fall of snow. These were followed by the young prince, who was dressed in a long piece of yellow cloth, wrapped loosely around him, and decorated with small bells, with a cap on his head to which was fastened a curious mask in imitation of a wolf's head, while the rear was brought up by the king himself in his robe of sea-otter skin, with a small whistle in his mouth and a rattle in his hand, with which he kept time to a sort of tune on his whistle. After passing very rapidly in this order around the house, each of them seated himself, except the prince, who immediately began his dance, which principally consisted in springing up into the air in a squat posture, and constantly turning around on his heels with great swiftness in a very narrow circle.

This dance, with a few intervals of rest, was continued for about two hours, during which the chiefs kept up a constant drumming with sticks of about a foot in length on a long hollow plank, which was, though a very noisy, a most doleful kind of music. This they accompanied with songs, the king himself acting as chorister, while the women applauded each feat of activity in the dancer, by repeating the words, *Wocash! Wocash Tyee!*[1] that is, Good! very good, Prince!

[1] The words were really *Waw-kash* (a word of salutation) and *Tyee*. This is in most common use in Nootka Sound. The order of salutation to a man is *Quaache-is*, to a woman *Chè-is*, and at parting *Klach-she*. A married woman is *Klootsnah*; a young girl *Hah-quatl-is*; an unmarried woman (whether old or young) *Hah-quatl*—distinctions which Jewitt does not make in his brief vocabulary. The Indians have many words to

As soon as the dance was finished, Maquina began to give presents to the strangers, in the name of his son Sat-sat-sok-sis. These were pieces of European cloth, generally of a fathom in length, muskets, powder, shot, etc. Whenever he gave them anything, they had a peculiar manner of snatching it from him with a very stern and surly look, repeating each time the words, *Wocash Tyee*. This I understood to be their custom, and was considered as a compliment, which, if omitted, would be supposed as a mark of disregard for the present. On this occasion Maquina gave away no less than one hundred muskets, the same number of looking-glasses, four hundred yards of cloth, and twenty casks of powder, besides other things.

After receiving these presents, the strangers retired on board their canoes, for so numerous were they that Maquina would not suffer any but the chiefs to sleep in the houses; and, in order to prevent the property from being pillaged by them, he ordered Thompson and myself to keep guard during the night, armed with cutlasses and pistols.

In this manner tribes of savages from various parts of the coast continued coming for several days, bringing with them blubber, oil, herring spawn, dried fish, and clams, for which they received in return presents of cloth, etc., after which they in general immediately returned home. I observed that very few, if any, of them, except the chiefs, had arms, which, I afterwards

express varieties of the same action. Thus *páttēs* means to wash. But *páttēe* is to wash all over; *tsont-soomik*, to wash the hands; *tsocuks*, to wash a pan, etc. *Haouwith*, or *Hawilth*, is the original word for chief, though *Tyee* is commonly used.

6

learned, is the custom with these people, whenever they come upon a friendly visit or to trade, in order to show, on their approach, that their intentions are pacific.[1]

[1] This is one of the earliest—if not the first—account of these periodical givings away of property so characteristic of the North-Western coast Indians, and known to the whites as "Potlatches." An Indian accumulates blankets and other portable property simply to give away at such feasts. Then if a poor, he becomes a great man, and even a kind of minor chief —a Life Peer, as it were. But those who have received much are expected to return the compliment by also giving a "potlatch," to which guests come from far and near. I have described one of these in *The Races of Mankind* (the first edition of *The Peoples of the World*), vol. i. pp. 75–90.

CHAPTER V

BURNING OF THE VESSEL—COMMENCEMENT OF JEWITT'S JOURNAL

EARLY on the morning of the 19th the ship was discovered to be on fire. This was owing to one of the savages having gone on board with a firebrand at night for the purpose of plunder, some sparks from which fell into the hold, and, communicating with some combustibles, soon enveloped the whole in flames. The natives regretted the loss of the ship the more as a great part of her cargo still remained on board. To my companion and myself it was a most melancholy sight, for with her disappeared from our eyes every trace of a civilised country; but the disappointment we experienced was still more severely felt, for we had calculated on having the provision to ourselves, which would have furnished us with a stock for years, as whatever is cured with salt, together with most of our other articles of food, are never eaten by these people. I had luckily saved all my tools, excepting the anvil and the bellows, which was attached to the forge, and from their weight had not been brought on shore. We had also the good fortune, in looking over what had been taken from the ship, to discover a box of chocolate and a case of port wine, which, as the Indians were not fond of it, proved

a great comfort to us for some time; and from one of
the natives I obtained a Nautical Almanack which had
belonged to the captain, and which was of great use to
me in determining the time.

About two days after, on examining their booty, the
savages found a tierce of rum, with which they were
highly delighted, as they have become very fond
of spirituous liquors since their intercourse with the
whites.[1] This was towards evening, and Maquina, having assembled all the men at his house, gave a feast, at
which they drank so freely of the rum, that in a short
time they became so extremely wild and frantic that
Thompson and myself, apprehensive for our safety,
thought it prudent to retire privately into the woods,
where we continued till past midnight.

On our return we found the women gone, who are
always very temperate, drinking nothing but water,
having quitted the house and gone to the other huts to
sleep, so terrified were they at the conduct of the men,
who lay all stretched out on the floor in a state of complete intoxication. How easy in this situation would
it have been for us to have dispatched or made ourselves
masters of our enemies had there been any ship near to
which we could have escaped, but as we were situated
the attempt would have been madness. The wish of
revenge was, however, less strongly impressed on my
mind than what appeared to be so evident an interposition of Divine Providence in our favour. How little can
man penetrate its designs, and how frequently is that

---

[1] It was about this date that Long, an Indian trader, described rum as
the *unum necessarium* for traffic with the savages. It is still eagerly
asked for, though its sale or gift is illegal.

intended as a blessing which he views as a curse. The burning of our ship, which we had lamented so much, as depriving us of so many comforts, now appeared to us in a very different light, for, had the savages got possession of the rum, of which there were nearly twenty puncheons on board,[1] we must inevitably have fallen a sacrifice to their fury in some of their moments of intoxication. This cask, fortunately, and a case of gin, was all the spirits they obtained from the ship. To prevent the recurrence of similar danger, I examined the cask, and, finding still a considerable quantity remaining, I bored a small hole in the bottom with a gimblet, which before morning, to my great joy, completely emptied it.

By this time the wound in my head began to be much better, so that I could enjoy some sleep, which I had been almost deprived of by the pain, and though I was still feeble from the loss of blood and my sufferings, I found myself sufficiently well to go to work at my trade, in making for the king and his wives bracelets and other small ornaments of copper or steel, and in repairing the arms, making use of a large square stone for the anvil, and heating my metal in a common wood fire. This was very gratifying to Maquina, and his women particularly, and secured me their goodwill.

In the meantime, great numbers from the other tribes kept continually flocking to Nootka, bringing with them, in exchange for the ship's plunder, such quantities of provision, that, notwithstanding the little success that Maquina met with in whaling this season, and their gluttonous waste, always eating to excess when they

---

[1] For sale, of course, to the Indians.

have it, regardless of the morrow, seldom did the natives experience any want of food during the summer. As to myself and companion, we fared as they did, never wanting for such provision as they had, though we were obliged to eat it cooked in their manner, and with train-oil as a sauce, a circumstance not a little unpleasant, both from their uncleanly mode of cooking and many of the articles of their food, which to a European are very disgusting; but, as the saying is, hunger will break through stone walls, and we found, at times, in the blubber of sea animals and the flesh of the dog-fish, loathsome as it generally was, a very acceptable repast.

But much oftener would poor Thompson, who was no favourite with them, have suffered from hunger had it not been for my furnishing him with provision. This I was enabled to do from my work, Maquina allowing me the privilege, when not employed for him, to work for myself in making bracelets and other ornaments of copper, fish-hooks, daggers, etc., either to sell to the tribes who visited us or for our own chiefs, who on these occasions, besides supplying me with as much as I wished to eat, and a sufficiency for Thompson, almost always made me a present of a European garment, taken from the ship, or some fathoms of cloth, which were made up by my comrade, and enabled us to go comfortably clad for some time; or small bundles of penknives, razors, scissors, etc., for one of which we could almost always procure from the natives two or three fresh salmon, cod, or halibut; or dried fish, clams, and herring spawn from the stranger tribes; and had we only been permitted to cook them after our own way, as we had pots and other utensils belonging to the ship, we should not have had much cause of complaint in this respect; but so tenacious are these people of their customs, particularly in the article of food and cooking, that the king always obliged me to give whatever provision I bought to the women to cook. And one day, finding Thompson and myself on the shore employed in boiling down sea-water into salt, on being told what it was he was very much displeased, and, taking the little we had procured, threw it into the sea. In one instance alone, as a particular favour, he allowed me to boil some salmon in my own way, when I invited him and his queen to eat with me; they tasted it, but did not like it, and made their meal of some of it that I had cooked in their country fashion.

In May the weather became uncommonly mild and pleasant, and so forward was vegetation, that I picked plenty of strawberries[1] by the middle of the month. Of this fruit there are great quantities on this coast, and I found them a most delicious treat.

My health now had become almost re-established, my wound being so far healed that it gave me no further trouble. I had never failed to wash it regularly once a day in sea water, and to dress it with a fresh leaf of tobacco, which I obtained from the natives, who had taken it from the ship, but made no use of it. This was all the dressing I gave it, except applying to it two or three times a little loaf sugar, which Maquina gave me, in order to remove some proud flesh, which prevented it from closing.

My cure would doubtless have been much sooner effected had I have been in a civilised country, where I

[1] Chiefly *Fragaria chilensis*.

could have had it dressed by a surgeon and properly attended to. But alas! I had no good Samaritan, with oil and wine, to bind up my wounds, and fortunate might I even esteem myself that I was permitted to dress it myself, for the utmost that I could expect from the natives was compassion for my misfortunes, which I indeed experienced from the women, particularly the queen, or favourite wife of Maquina, the mother of Sat-sat-sok-sis, who used frequently to point to my head, and manifest much kindness and solicitude for me. I must do Maquina the justice to acknowledge, that he always appeared desirous of sparing me any labour which he believed might be hurtful to me, frequently inquiring in an affectionate manner if my head pained me. As for the others, some of the chiefs excepted, they cared little what became of me, and probably would have been gratified with my death.

My health being at length re-established and my wound healed, Thompson became very importunate for me to begin my journal, and as I had no ink, proposed to cut his finger to supply me with blood for the purpose whenever I should want it. On the 1st of June I accordingly commenced a regular diary, but had no occasion to make use of the expedient suggested by my comrade, having found a much better substitute in the expressed juice of a certain plant, which furnished me with a bright green colour, and, after making a number of trials, I at length succeeded in obtaining a very tolerable ink, by boiling the juice of the blackberry with a mixture of finely powdered charcoal, and filtering it through a cloth. This I afterwards preserved in bottles, and found it answer very well, so true is it that " necessity

is the mother of invention." As for quills, I found no
difficulty in procuring them whenever I wanted, from
the crows and ravens with which the beach was almost
always covered, attracted by the offal of whales, seals,
etc., and which were so tame that I could easily kill them
with stones, while a large clam-shell furnished me with
an inkstand.

The extreme solicitude of Thompson that I should
begin my journal might be considered as singular in a
man who neither knew how to read or write, a circumstance, by the way, very uncommon in an American,
were we less acquainted with the force of habit, he
having been for many years at sea, and accustomed to
consider the keeping of a journal as a thing indispensable. This man was born in Philadelphia, and at eight
years old ran away from his friends and entered as a
cabin boy on board a ship bound to London. On his
arrival there, finding himself in distress, he engaged as
an apprentice to the captain of a collier, from whence
he was impressed on board an English man-of-war, and
continued in the British naval service about twenty-
seven years, during which he was present at the engage-
ment under Lord Howe with the French fleet in June
1794, and when peace was made between England
and France, was discharged. He was a very strong
and powerful man, an expert boxer, and perfectly
fearless; indeed, so little was his dread of danger,
that when irritated he was wholly regardless of his
life. Of this the following will furnish a sufficient
proof:—

One evening about the middle of April, as I was at
the house of one of the chiefs, where I had been

employed on some work for him, word was brought me that Maquina was going to kill Thompson. I immediately hurried home, where I found the king in the act of presenting a loaded musket at Thompson, who was standing before him with his breast bared and calling on him to fire. I instantly stepped up to Maquina, who was foaming with rage, and, addressing him in soothing words, begged him for my sake not to kill my father, and at length succeeded in taking the musket from him and persuading him to sit down.

On inquiring into the cause of his anger, I learned that, while Thompson was lighting the lamps in the king's room, Maquina having substituted ours for their pine torches, some of the boys began to tease him, running around him and pulling him by the trousers, among the most forward of whom was the young prince. This caused Thompson to spill the oil, which threw him into such a passion, that, without caring what he did, he struck the prince so violent a blow in his face with his fist as to knock him down. The sensation excited among the savages by an act which was considered as the highest indignity, and a profanation of the sacred person of majesty, may be easily conceived. The king was immediately acquainted with it, who, on coming in and seeing his son's face covered with blood, seized a musket and began to load it, determined to take instant revenge of the audacious offender, and had I arrived a few moments later than I did, my companion would certainly have paid with his life for his rash and violent conduct. I found the utmost difficulty in pacifying Maquina, who for a long time after could not forgive

Thompson, but would repeatedly say, "John, *you* die—Thompson kill."

But to appease the king was not all that was necessary. In consequence of the insult offered to their prince, the whole tribe held a council, in which it was unanimously resolved that Thompson should be put to death in the most cruel manner. I however interceded so strenuously with Maquina for his life, telling him that if my father was killed, I was determined not to survive him, that he refused to deliver him up to the vengeance of his people, saying, that for John's sake they must consent to let him live. The prince, who, after I had succeeded in calming his father, gave me an account of what had happened, told me that it was wholly out of regard to me, as Thompson was my father, that his life had been spared, for that if any one of the tribe should dare to lift a hand against him in anger, he would most certainly be put to death.

Yet even this narrow escape produced not much effect on Thompson, or induced him to restrain the violence of his temper. For, not many weeks after, he was guilty of a similar indiscretion, in striking the eldest son of a chief, who was about eighteen years old, and, according to their custom, was considered as a Tyee, or chief, himself, in consequence of his having provoked him by calling him a white slave. This affair caused great commotion in the village, and the tribe was very clamorous for his death, but Maquina would not consent.

I used frequently to remonstrate with him on the imprudence of his conduct, and beg him to govern his temper better, telling him that it was our duty, since our lives were in the power of these savages, to do nothing to exasperate them. But all I could say on this point availed little, for so bitter was the hate he felt for them, which he was no way backward in manifesting both by his looks and actions, that he declared he never would submit to their insults, and that he had much rather be killed than be obliged to live among them; adding that he only wished he had a good vessel and some guns, and he would destroy the whole of the cursed race; for to a brave sailor like him, who had fought the French and Spaniards with glory, it was a punishment worse than death to be a slave to such a poor, ignorant, despicable set of beings.

As for myself, I thought very differently. After returning thanks to that merciful Being who had in so wonderful a manner softened the hearts of the savages in my favour, I had determined from the first of my capture to adopt a conciliating conduct towards them, and conform myself, as far as was in my power, to their customs and mode of thinking, trusting that the same divine goodness that had rescued me from death, would not always suffer me to languish in captivity among these heathens.

With this view, I sought to gain their good-will by always endeavouring to assume a cheerful countenance, appearing pleased with their sports and buffoon tricks, making little ornaments for the wives and children of their chiefs, by which means I became quite a favourite with them, and fish-hooks, daggers, etc., for themselves.

As a further recommendation to their favour, and what might eventually prove of the utmost importance to us, I resolved to learn their language, which in the course of a few months' residence I so far succeeded in acquiring, as to be able in general to make myself well understood.

I likewise tried to persuade Thompson to learn it, as what might prove necessary to him. But he refused, saying that he hated both them and their cursed lingo, and would have nothing to do with it.

By pursuing this conciliatory plan, so far did I gain the good-will of these savages, particularly the chiefs, that I scarcely ever failed experiencing kind treatment from them, and was received with a smile of welcome at their houses, where I was always sure of having something given me to eat, whenever they had it, and many a good meal have I had from them, when they themselves were short of provisions and suffering for the want of them.

And it was a common practice with me, when we had nothing to eat at home, which happened not unfrequently during my stay among them, to go around the village, and on noticing a smoke from any of the houses, which denoted that they were cooking, enter in without ceremony, and ask them for something, which I was never refused.

Few nations, indeed, are there so very rude and unfeeling, whom constant mild treatment, and an attention to please, will not mollify and obtain from some return of kind attention. This the treatment I received from these people may exemplify, for not numerous, even among those calling themselves civilised, are there instances to be found of persons depriving themselves of food to give it to a stranger, whatever may be his merits.

It may perhaps be as well in this place to give a description of Nootka; some accounts of the tribes who were accustomed to visit us; and the manners and customs of the people, as far as I hitherto had an opportunity of observing them.

CHAPTER VI

DESCRIPTION OF NOOTKA SOUND—MANNER OF BUILD-ING HOUSES—FURNITURE—DRESSES

THE village of Nootka is situated in between 49 and
50 deg. N. lat.,[1] at the bottom of Friendly Cove, on the
west or north-west side.   It consists of about twenty
houses or huts, on a small hill, which rises with a gentle
ascent from the shore.   Friendly Cove, which affords
good and secure anchorage for ships close in with the
shore, is a small harbour of not more than a quarter or
half a mile in length, and about half a mile or three-
quarters broad, formed by the line of coast on the east
and a long point or headland, which extends as much
as three leagues into the Sound, in nearly a westerly
direction.[2]   This, as well as I can judge from what I
have seen of it, is in general from one to two miles in
breadth, and mostly a rocky and unproductive soil, with

---

[1] The exact position of the village is lat. 49° 35′ 31″ N. ; long. 126°
37′ 32″ W.

[2] According to the Admiralty Sailing Directions, the Cove is about two
cables in extent, and sheltered from the sea by a small rocky high-water
island on its east side.   It affords anchorage in the middle for only one
vessel of moderate size, though several small vessels might find shelter.
When Vancouver visited it in 1792, no less than eight ships were in it,
most of them small, and secured to the shore by hawsers.

but few trees. The eastern and western shores of this harbour are steep and in many parts rocky, the trees growing quite to the water's edge, but the bottom to the north and north-west is a fine sandy beach of half a mile or more in extent.

From the village to the north and north-east extends a plain, the soil of which is very excellent, and with proper cultivation may be made to produce almost any of our European vegetables ; this is but little more than half a mile in breadth, and is terminated by the sea-coast, which in this place is lined with rocks and reefs, and cannot be approached by ships. The coast in the neighbourhood of Nootka is in general low, and but little broken into hills and valleys. The soil is good, well covered with fine forests of pine, spruce, beech, and other trees, and abounds with streams of the finest water, the general appearance being the same for many miles around.

The village is situated on the ground occupied by the Spaniards, when they kept a garrison here ; the foundations of the church and the governor's house are yet visible, and a few European plants are still to be found, which continue to be self-propagated, such as onions, peas, and turnips, but the two last are quite small, particularly the turnips, which afforded us nothing but the tops for eating. Their former village stood on the same spot, but the Spaniards, finding it a commodious situation, demolished the houses, and forced the inhabitants to retire five or six miles into the country.[1] With

---

[1] This means farther up the Sound ; for there are villages in the interior of Vancouver Island. The Admiralty Sailing Directions declare that not a trace of the Spanish settlement now exists. This is scarcely correct,

7

HABITATIONS IN NOOTKA SOUND.

great sorrow, as Maquina told me, did they find themselves compelled to quit their ancient place of residence,
but with equal joy did they repossess themselves of
it when the Spanish garrison was expelled by the
English.

The houses, as I have observed, are above twenty in
number, built nearly in a line. These are of different
sizes, according to the rank or quality of the *Tyee*, or
chief, who lives in them, each having one, of which he is
considered as the lord. They vary not much in width,
being usually from thirty-six to forty feet wide, but are
of very different lengths, that of the king, which is much
the longest, being about one hundred and fifty feet,
while the smallest, which contain only two families, do
not exceed forty feet in length; the house of the king is
also distinguished from the others by being higher.

Their method of building is as follows: they erect in
the ground two very large posts, at such a distance apart
as is intended for the length of the house. On these,
which are of equal height, and hollowed out at the upper
end, they lay a large spar for the ridge-pole of the build-

---

for an indistinct ridge shows the site of houses, and here and there a few
bricks half hidden in the ground may be detected.   I have seen a cannon
ball and a Mexican dollar found there.   Many of the Nootka Indians have
large moustaches and whiskers, which may possibly be due to their
Spanish blood, and others were decidedly Chinese-looking, a fact which
may be traced to the presence of Meares's Chinese carpenters in 1778–79.
Some of them can, or could, thirty years ago, by tradition, count ten
in Spanish; and there is a legend in the Sound to the effect that the
white men had begun to cultivate the ground, and to erect a stockade and
fort; when one day a ship came with papers for the head man, who was
observed to cry, and all the foreigners became sad.   The next day they
began moving their goods to the ship.   But, as Mr. Sproat suggests, this
might have reference to Meares's settlement.

ing, or, if the length of the house requires it, two or more,
supporting their ends by similar upright posts; these
spars are sometimes of an almost incredible size,
having myself measured one in Maquina's house, which
I found to be one hundred feet long and eight feet four
inches in circumference. At equal distances from these
two posts, two others are placed on each side, to form
the width of the building; these are rather shorter than
the first, and on them are laid in like manner spars, but
of a smaller size, having the upper part hewed flat, with
a narrow ridge on the outer side to support the ends of
the planks.

The roof is formed of pine planks with a broad feather
edge, so as to lap well over each other, which are laid
lengthwise from the ridge-pole in the centre, to the
beams at the sides, after which the top is covered with
planks of eight feet broad, which form a kind of coving
projecting so far over the ends of the planks that form
the roof, as completely to exclude the rain. On these
they lay large stones to prevent their being displaced
by the wind. The ends of the planks are not secured
to the beams on which they are laid by any fastening,
so that in a high storm I have often known all the men
obliged to turn out and go upon the roof to prevent
them from being blown off, carrying large stones and
pieces of rock with them to secure the boards, always
stripping themselves naked on these occasions, whatever
may be the severity of the weather, to prevent their
garments from being wet and muddied, as these storms
are almost always accompanied with heavy rains. The
sides of their houses are much more open and exposed
to the weather; this proceeds from their not being so

easily made close as the roof, being built with planks of
about ten feet long and four or five wide, which they
place between stancheons or small posts of the height
of the roof; of these there are four to each range of
boards, two at each end, and so near each other as to
leave space enough for admitting a plank. The planks
or boards which they make use of for building their
houses, and for other uses, they procure of different
lengths as occasion requires, by splitting them out
with hard wooden wedges from pine logs, and afterwards dubbing them down with their chisels, with much
patience, to the thickness wanted, rendering them quite
smooth.

There is but one entrance; this is placed usually at
the end, though sometimes in the middle, as was that of
Maquina's. Through the middle of the building, from
one end to the other, runs a passage of about eight or
nine feet broad, on each side of which the several
families that occupy it live, each having its particular
fireplace, but without any kind of wall or separation to
mark their respective limits; the chief having his apartment at the upper end, and the next in rank opposite
on the other side. They have no other floor than the
ground; the fireplace or hearth consists of a number of
stones loosely put together, but they are wholly without
a chimney, nor is there any opening left in the roof, but
whenever a fire is made, the plank immediately over it
is thrust aside, by means of a pole, to give vent to the
smoke.

The height of the houses in general, from the ground
to the centre of the roof, does not exceed ten feet, that of
Maquina's was not far from fourteen; the spar forming

the ridge-pole of the latter was painted in red and black circles alternately, by way of ornament, and the large posts that supported it had their tops curiously wrought or carved, so as to represent human heads of a monstrous size, which were painted in their manner. These were not, however, considered as objects of adoration, but merely as ornaments.[1]

The furniture of these people is very simple, and consists only of boxes, in which they put their clothes, furs, and such things as they hold most valuable; tubs for keeping their provisions of spawn and blubber in; trays from which they eat; baskets for their dried fish and other purposes, and bags made of bark matting, of which they also make their beds, spreading a piece of it upon the ground when they lie down, and using no other bed covering than their garments. The boxes are of pine, with a top that shuts over, and instead of nails or pegs, are fastened with flexible twigs; they are extremely smooth and high polished, and sometimes ornamented with rows of very small white shells. The tubs are of a square form, secured in the like manner, and of various sizes, some being extremely large, having seen them that were six feet long by four broad and five deep. The trays are hollowed out with their chisels from a solid block of wood, and the baskets and mats are made from the bark of trees.

From bark they likewise make the cloth for their garments, in the following manner:—A quantity of this bark is taken and put into fresh water, where it is kept for a fortnight, to give it time to completely soften;

---

[1] This is a good description of the house of Maquina's grandson, as I saw it fifty-eight years after Jewitt's time.

INTERIOR OF A HABITATION IN NOOTKA SOUND.

it is then taken out and beaten upon a plank, with an instrument made of bone, or some very hard wood, having grooves or hollows on one side of it, care being taken to keep the mass constantly moistened with water, in order to separate, with more ease, the hard and woody from the soft and fibrous parts, which, when completed, they parcel out into skeins, like thread. These they lay in the air to bleach, and afterwards dye them black or red, as suits their fancies, their natural colour being a pale yellow. In order to form the cloth, the women, by whom the whole of this process is performed, take a certain number of these skeins and twist them together, by rolling them with their hands upon their knees into hard rolls, which are afterwards connected by means of a strong thread, made for the purpose.

Their dress usually consists of but a single garment, which is a loose cloak or mantle (called *kutsack*) in one piece, reaching nearly to the feet. This is tied loosely over the right or left shoulder, so as to leave the arms at full liberty.

Those of the common people are painted red with ochre the better to keep out the rain, but the chiefs wear them of their native colour, which is a pale yellow, ornamenting them with borders of the sea-otter skin, a kind of grey cloth made of the hair of some animal [1] which they procure from the tribes to the south, or their own cloth wrought or painted with various figures in red or black, representing men's heads, the sun and moon, fish and animals, which are frequently executed

[1] Dog's hair. A tribe on Fraser River used to keep flocks of these curs, which they periodically clipped like sheep.

with much skill. They have also a girdle of the same kind for securing this mantle or *kutsack* around them, which is in general still more highly ornamented, and serves them to wear their daggers and knives in. In winter, however, they sometimes make use of an additional garment, which is a kind of hood, with a hole in it for the purpose of admitting the head, and falls over the breast and back, as low as the shoulders; this is bordered both at top and bottom with fur, and is never worn except when they go out.

The garments of the women vary not essentially from those of the men, the mantle having holes in it for the purpose of admitting the arms, and being tied close under the chin instead of over the shoulder. The chiefs have also mantles of the sea-otter skin, but these are only put on upon extraordinary occasions; and one that is made from the skin of a certain large animal, which is brought from the south by the Wickanninish[1] and Kla-iz-zarts.[2] This they prepare by dressing it in warm water, scraping off the hair and what flesh adheres to it carefully with sharp mussel-shells, and spreading it out in the sun to dry on a wooden frame, so as to preserve the shape. When dressed in this manner it becomes perfectly white, and as pliable as the best deer's leather, but almost as thick again. They then paint it in different figures with such paints as they usually employ in decorating their persons; these figures mostly represent human heads, canoes employed in catching whales, etc.

This skin is called metamelth, and is probably got

---

[1] Probably the Klayoquahts (see p. 77).
[2] Klahosahts.

from an animal of the moose kind ; it is highly prized by
these people, is their great war dress, and only worn
when they wish to make the best possible display of
themselves. Strips or bands of it, painted as above, are
also sometimes used by them for girdles or the border-
ing of their cloaks, and also for bracelets and ankle
ornaments by some of the inferior class.

On their heads, when they go out upon any excursion,
particularly whaling or fishing, they wear a kind of cap
or bonnet in form not unlike a large sugar loaf with the
top cut off. This is made of the same materials with
their cloth,[1] but is in general of a closer texture, and
by way of tassel has a long strip of the skin of the
metamelth[2] attached to it, covered with rows of small
white shells or beads. Those worn by the common
people are painted entirely red, the chiefs having theirs
of different colours. The one worn by the king, and
which serves to designate him from all the others, is
longer and broader at the bottom ; the top, instead of
being flat, having upon it an ornament in the figure
of a small urn. It is also of a much finer texture
than the others, and plaited or wrought in black and
white stripes, with the representation in front of a canoe
in pursuit of a whale, with the harpooner standing in

---

[1] The outside is made of cedar bark, the inside of white-hair bark.

[2] I have more than once discussed the identity of this animal with
Indian traders. None of them recognised it, nor, indeed, were acquainted
with the animal by the name Jewitt applies to it. It is, however, not
unlikely the North-Western marmot (*Arctomys pruinosus*), specimens
of which are now and then—though, it must be admitted, rarely—seen in
Vancouver Island ; but it is more common farther south. The Alberni
Indians (Seshahts and Opechesahts) used to talk of a beast called *Sit-si-
tehl*, which we took to be the marmot, and Mr. Sproat saw one ; I was
not so fortunate.

the prow prepared to strike. This bonnet is called *Seeya-poks.*

Their mode of living is very simple—their food consisting almost wholly of fish, or fish spawn fresh or dried, the blubber of the whale, seal, or sea-cow, mussels, clams, and berries of various kinds; all of which are eaten with a profusion of train-oil for sauce, not excepting even the most delicate fruit, as strawberries and raspberries.

With so little variety in their food, no great secret can be expected in their cookery. Of this, indeed, they may be said to know but two methods, viz. by boiling and steaming, and even the latter is not very frequently practised by them. Their mode of boiling is as follows :—Into one of their tubs they pour water sufficient to cook the quantity of provision wanted. A number of heated stones are then put in to make it boil, when the salmon or other fish are put in without any other preparation than sometimes cutting off the heads, tails, and fins, the boiling in the meantime being kept up by the application of the hot stones, after which it is left to cook until the whole is nearly reduced to one mass. It is then taken out and distributed in the trays. In a similar manner they cook their blubber and spawn, smoked or dried fish, and, in fine, almost everything they eat, nothing going down with them like broth.

When they cook their fish by steam, which are usually the heads, tails, and fins of the salmon, cod, and halibut, a large fire is kindled, upon which they place a bed of stones, which, when the wood is burnt down, becomes perfectly heated. Layers of green leaves or pine boughs are then placed upon the stones, and the fish, clams, etc., being laid upon them, water is poured over them, and the whole closely covered with mats to keep in the steam. This is much the best mode of cooking, and clams and mussels done in this manner are really excellent.[1] These, as I have said, may be considered as their only kinds of cookery; though I have, in a very few instances, known them dress the roe or spawn of the salmon and the herring, when first taken, in a different manner; this was by roasting them, the former being supported between two split pieces of pine, and the other having a sharp stick run through it, with one end fixed in the ground; sprats are also roasted by them in this way, a number being spitted upon one stick; and this kind of food, with a little salt, would be found no contemptible eating even to an European.

At their meals they seat themselves upon the ground, with their feet curled up under them, around their trays, which are generally about three feet long by one broad, and from six to eight inches deep. In eating they make use of nothing but their fingers, except for the soup or oil, which they lade out with clam-shells.

Around one of these trays from four to six persons will seat themselves, constantly dipping in their fingers or clam-shells one after the other. The king and chiefs alone have separate trays, from which no one is permitted to eat with them except the queen, or principal wife of the chief; and whenever the king or one of the

---

[1] In the opinion of the judicious Jewitt, every one who has eaten food—especially salmon and shell-fish—cooked after this fashion will coincide. *Experto crede.*

chiefs wishes to distinguish any of his people with a special mark of favour on these occasions, he calls him and gives him some of the choice bits from his tray. The slaves eat at the same time, and of the same provisions, faring in this respect as well as their masters, being seated with the family, and only feeding from separate trays.

Whenever a feast is given by the king or any of the chiefs, there is a person who acts as a master of ceremonies, and whose business it is to receive the guests as they enter the house, and point out to them their respective seats, which is regulated with great punctiliousness as regards rank; the king occupying the highest or the seat of honour, his son or brother sitting next him, and so on with the chiefs according to their quality; the private persons belonging to the same family being always placed together, to prevent any confusion. The women are seldom invited to their feasts, and only at those times when a general invitation is given to the village.[1]

As, whenever they cook, they always calculate to have an abundance for all the guests, a profusion in this respect being considered as the highest luxury, much more is usually set before them than they can eat. That which is left in the king's tray, he sends to his house for his family by one of his slaves, as do the chiefs theirs; while those who eat from the same tray, and who generally belong to the same family, take it home as common stock, or each one receives his portion, which is distributed on the spot. This custom appeared

---

[1] Or to one or more of the neighbouring tribes, such feasts being known as *Wawkoahs*.

very singular to my companion and myself, and it was a most awkward thing for us, at first, to have to lug home with us, in our hands or arms, the blubber of fish that we received at these times, but we soon became reconciled to it, and were very glad of an opportunity to do it.

NOOTKA SOUND INDIANS.

CHAPTER VII

APPEARANCE OF THE NATIVES — ORNAMENTS —
OTTER-HUNTING — FISHING — CANOES

IN point of personal appearance the people of Nootka
are among the best-looking of any of the tribes that I
have seen. The men are in general from about five feet
six to five feet eight inches in height; remarkably straight,
of a good form, robust and strong, with their limbs in
general well turned and proportioned, excepting the
legs and feet, which are clumsy and ill formed, owing,
no doubt, to their practice of sitting on them, though
I have seen instances in which they were very well
shaped; this defect is more particularly apparent in the
women, who are for the most part of the time within
doors, and constantly sitting while employed in their
cooking and other occupations.[1] The only instance of

[1] Yet they are by no means weak in the legs, a coast Indian being
capable of long travel in the bush without tiring. The Hydahs of Queen
Charlotte Island, and the Tlinkets and Kaloshes of the neighbouring
mainland, are splendid specimens of men, tall, comparatively fair, large-
headed, regularly-featured, and endowed with courage and intelligence,
though their morals leave much to be desired. All the canoe Indians
are very strong-handed, owing to the constant use of the paddle. In a
scuffle with one of them, it does not do to let him get a grip ; better
prevent him from coming to close quarters, for in this case the white man
has little chance. The Klahoquahts are the finest-looking of the Vancouver
west coast tribes.

deformity that I saw amongst them was a man of dwarfish stature ; he was thirty years old, and but three feet three inches high ; he had, however, no other defect than his diminutive size, being well made, and as strong and able to bear fatigue as what they were in general.[1]

Their complexion, when freed from the paint and oil with which their skins are generally covered, is a brown, somewhat inclining to a copper cast. The shape of the face is oval ; the features are tolerably regular, the lips being thin and the teeth very white and even ; their eyes are black but rather small, and the nose pretty well formed, being neither flat nor very prominent ; their hair is black, long, and coarse, but they have no beard, completely extirpating it, as well as the hair from their bodies, Maquina being the only exception, who suffered his beard to grow on his upper lip in the manner of mustachios, which was considered as a mark of dignity.

As to the women, they are much whiter, many of them not being darker than those in some of the southern parts of Europe. They are in general very well - looking, and some quite handsome. Maquina's favourite wife in particular, who was a Wickinninish princess, would be considered as a beautiful woman in

---

[1] I have rarely seen a corpulent Indian, and not one idiot, or a cripple so deformed that he was incapable of earning his livelihood. It is seldom that they are deformed from birth, and when they are, they generally disappear, so as not to be a burden on the tribe. As a facetious old savage remarked to me, when discussing that curious immunity from helplessness in his tribe, "The climate doesn't agree with them." The brother of Quisto, chief of the Pachenahts in 1865 (San Juan Harbour), was much deformed in the legs, but he was an excellent canoeman.

8

any country. She was uncommonly well formed, tall, and of a majestic appearance; her skin remarkably fair for one of these people, with considerable colour, her features handsome, and her eyes black, soft, and languishing; her hair was very long, thick, and black, as is that of the females in general, which is much softer than that of the men; in this they take much pride, frequently oiling and plaiting it carefully into two broad plaits, tying the ends with a strip of the cloth of the country, and letting it hang down before on each side of the face.

The women keep their garments much neater and cleaner than the men, and are extremely modest in their deportment and dress; their mantle, or *kutsack*, which is longer than that of the men, reaching quite to their feet and completely enveloping them, being tied close under the chin, and bound with a girdle of the same cloth or of sea-otter skin around their waists; it has also loose sleeves, which reach to the elbows. Though fond of ornamenting their persons, they are by no means so partial to paint as the men, merely colouring their eyebrows black and drawing a bright red stripe from each corner of the mouth towards the ear. Their ornaments consist chiefly of ear-rings, necklaces, bracelets, rings for the fingers and ankles, and small nose-jewels (the latter are, however, wholly confined to the wives of the king or chiefs); these are principally made out of copper or brass, highly polished and of various forms and sizes; the nose-jewel is usually a small white shell[1] or bead suspended to a thread.

[1] Commonly the flattish nacreous portion of the Abelone, or Ear-shell (*Haliotis Kamschatkiana*), known as *Apats-em*, which is pawned or sold

The wives of the common people frequently wear for bracelets and ankle rings strips of the country cloth or skin of the metamelth painted in figures, and those of the king or principal chiefs, bracelets and necklaces consisting of a number of strings of *Ife-waw*, an article much prized by them, and which makes a very handsome appearance. This *Ife-waw*, as they term it, is a kind of shell of a dazzling whiteness and as smooth as ivory; it is of a cylindrical form, in a slight degree curved, about the size of a goose quill, hollow, three inches in length and gradually tapering to a point, which is broken off by the natives as it is taken from the water; this they afterwards string upon threads of bark and sell it by the fathom; it forms a kind of circulating medium among these nations, five fathoms being considered as the price of a slave, their most valuable species of property. It is principally obtained from the Aitizzarts, a people living about thirty or forty miles to the northward, who collect it from the reefs and sunken rocks with which their coast abounds, though it is also brought in considerable quantity from the south.[1]

in times of scarcity. By constant removal and insertion, the septum of the nose, through which it is fastened, becomes in time so large that it will admit almost any kind of moderately-sized ornament. Feathers are frequently inserted, and more than once I have seen an Indian, clad in a blanket alone, denude himself of his single garment to hold biscuits or other goods, and dispose of his pipe by sticking it in the hole through his nasal septum, which, had times been better, would have been occupied with a piece of shell, either square, oblong, or of a horseshoe shape.

[1] This is the well-known *Dentalium pretiosum*, or Tooth-shell, generally known as the *Hioqua*. It is procured chiefly from Cape Flattery, on the southern side of Juan de Fuca Strait, and from Koskeemo Sound on the north. The "Aitizzarts" (Ayhuttisahts) probably obtained it by barter with the tribes on that part of the coast. It is not much used nowadays. —*The Peoples of the World*, vol. i. p. 60.

Their mode of taking it has been thus described to me:—To one end of a pole is fastened a piece of plank, in which a considerable number of pine pegs are inserted, made sharp at the ends; above the plank, in order to sink it, a stone or some weight is tied, and the other end of the pole suspended to a long rope; this is let down perpendicularly by the *Ife-waw* fishers in those places where that substance is found, which are usually from fifty to sixty fathoms deep. On finding the bottom, they raise the pole up a few feet and let it fall; this they repeat a number of times, as if sounding, when they draw it up and take off the *Ife-waw* which is found adhering to the points. This method of procuring it is very laborious and fatiguing, especially as they seldom take more than two or three of these shells at a time, and frequently none.

Though the women, as I have said, make but little use of paint, the very reverse is the case with the men. In decorating their heads and faces they place their principal pride, and none of our most fashionable beaus when preparing for a grand ball can be more particular; for I have known Maquina, after having been employed more than an hour in painting his face, rub the whole off, and recommence the operation anew, when it did not entirely please him.

The manner in which they paint themselves frequently varies, according to the occasion, but it oftener is the mere dictate of whim. The most usual method is to paint the eyebrows black in form of a half-moon and the face red in small squares, with the arms and legs and part of the body red; sometimes one half of the face is painted red in squares and the other black;

at others dotted with spots of red and black instead of squares, with a variety of other devices, such as painting one half of the face and body red and the other black.

But a method of painting which they sometimes employed, and which they were much more particular in, was by laying on the face a quantity of bear's grease of about one-eighth of an inch thick; this they raised up into ridges resembling a small bead in joiner's work with a stick prepared for the purpose, and then painted them red, which gave the face a very singular appearance.

On extraordinary occasions the king and principal chiefs used to strew over their faces, after painting, a fine black shining powder procured from some mineral, as Maquina told me it was got from the rocks. This they call *pelpelth*,[1] and value it highly, as, in their opinion, it serves to set off their looks to great advantage, glittering especially in the sun like silver. This article is brought them in bags by the *Newchemass*,[2] a very savage nation who live a long way to the north, from whom they likewise receive a superior kind of red paint, a species of very fine and rich ochre, which they hold in much estimation.

[1] This is powdered mica of the black variety. It is obtained in various places, from veins exposed, for the most part in the beds of streams.

[2] These seem to be the Nimpkish, from the Nimpkish River, south of Fort Rupert, on the eastern shore of Vancouver Island, who still frequently cross the island by a chain of rivers and lakes to Nootka Sound. This is confirmed by Jewitt writing in another place that they lived somewhat in the interior. It is doubtful whether he knew that the country in which he lived was an island. At all events, he never mentions it by that name. This route I have described in "Das Innere der Vancouver Insel" (Petermann, *Geographische Mittheilungen*, 1869).

Notwithstanding this custom of painting themselves, they make it an invariable practice, both in summer and winter, to bathe once a day, and sometimes oftener; but as the paint is put on with oil, it is not much discomposed thereby, and whenever they wish to wash it off, they repair to some piece of fresh water and scour themselves with sand or rushes.

In dressing their heads on occasion of a festival or a visit, they are full as particular and almost as long as in painting. The hair, after being well oiled, is carefully gathered upon the top of the head and secured by a piece of pine or spruce bough with the green leaves upon it. After having it properly fixed in this manner, the king and principal chiefs used to strew all over it the white down obtained from a species of large brown eagle which abounds on this coast, and which they are very particular in arranging so as not to have a single feather out of place, occasionally wetting the hair to make it adhere. This, together with the bough, which is sometimes of considerable size and stuck over with feathers by means of turpentine, gives them a very singular and grotesque appearance, which they, however, think very becoming, and the first thing they do, on learning the arrival of strangers, is to go and decorate themselves in this manner.

The men also wear bracelets of painted leather or copper and large earrings of the latter, but the ornament on which they appear to set the most value is the nose-jewel, if such an appellation may be given to the wooden stick which some of them employ for this purpose. The king and chiefs, however, wear them of a different form, being either small pieces of polished copper or brass, of

which I made many for them in the shape of hearts and
diamonds, or a twisted conical shell about half an inch
in length, of a bluish colour and very bright, which is
brought from the south. These are suspended by a
small wire or string to the hole in the gristle of the
nose, which is formed in infancy by boring it with a
pin, the hole being afterwards enlarged by the repeated
insertion of wooden pegs of an increased size, until
it becomes about the diameter of a pipe-stem, though
some have them of a size nearly sufficient to admit the
little finger.

The common class, who cannot readily procure the
more expensive jewels that I have mentioned, substitute
for them, usually, a smooth, round stick, some of which
are of an almost incredible length, for I have seen them
projecting not less than eight or nine inches beyond
the face on each side; this is made fast or secured in
its place by little wedges on each side of it. These
" sprit-sail-yard fellows," as my messmate used to call
them, when rigged out in this manner, made quite a
strange show, and it was his delight, whenever he saw
one of them coming towards us with an air of consequence proportioned to the length of his stick, to put
up his hand suddenly as he was passing him, so as to
strike the stick, in order, as he said, to brace him up
sharp to the wind; this used to make them very angry,
but nothing was more remote from Thompson's ideas
than a wish to cultivate their favour.

The natives of Nootka appear to have but little
inclination for the chase, though some of them were
expert marksmen, and used sometimes to shoot ducks
and geese; but the seal and the sea - otter form the

principal objects of their hunting, particularly the latter.

Of this animal, so much noted for its valuable skin, the following description may not be uninteresting:— The sea-otter[1] is nearly five feet in length, exclusive of the tail, which is about twelve inches, and is very thick and broad where it joins the body, but gradually tapers to the end, which is tipped with white. The colour of the rest is a shining, silky black, with the exception of a broad white stripe on the top of the head. Nothing can be more beautiful than one of these animals when seen swimming, especially when on the look-out for any object. At such times it raises its head quite above the surface, and the contrast between the shining black and the white, together with its sharp ears and a long tuft of hair rising from the middle of its forehead, which looks like three small horns, render it quite a novel and attractive object. They are in general very tame, and will permit a canoe or boat to approach very near before they dive. I was told, however, that they are become much more shy since they have been accustomed to shoot them with muskets, than when they used only arrows.[2]

The skin is held in great estimation in China, more especially that of the tail, the fur of which is finer and closer set than that on the body. This is always cut off and sold separately by the natives. The value of a skin is determined by its size, that being considered

---

[1] *Enhydra lutris*, or "Quiaotluck," now so rapidly decreasing in numbers that it can scarcely escape the fate of Steller's Rhytina.

[2] For an account of the habits and history of these valued animals, the reader is referred to *The Countries of the World*, vol. i. p. 304.

as a prime skin which will reach, in length, from a man's chin to his feet. The food of the sea-otter is fish, which he is very dexterous in taking, being an excellent swimmer, with feet webbed like those of a goose. They appear to be wholly confined to the sea-coast, at least to the salt water. They have usually three or four young at a time, but I know not how often they breed, nor in what place they deposit their young, though I have frequently seen them swimming around the mother when no larger than rats. The flesh is eaten by the natives, cooked in their usual mode by boiling, and is far preferable to that of the seal, of which they make much account.

But if not great hunters, there are few people more expert in fishing. Their lines are generally made from the sinew of the whale, and are extremely strong. For the hook, they usually make use of a straight piece of hard wood, in the lower part of which is inserted, and well secured with thread or whale sinew, a bit of bone made very sharp at the point and bearded; but I used to make for them hooks from iron, which they preferred, not only as being less liable to break, but more certain of securing the fish. Cod, halibut, and other sea fish were not only caught by them with hooks, but even salmon.

To take this latter fish, they practise the following method :—One person seats himself in a small canoe, and, baiting his hook with a sprat, which they are always careful to procure as fresh as possible, fastens his line to the handle of the paddle; this, as he plies it in the water, keeps the fish in constant motion, so as to give it the appearance of life, which the salmon seeing, leaps at it and is instantly hooked, and, by a sudden and dexterous motion of the paddle, drawn on board. I have known some of the natives take no less than eight or ten salmon of a morning, in this manner, and have seen from twenty to thirty canoes at a time in Friendly Cove thus employed.

They are likewise little less skilful in taking the whale. This they kill with a kind of javelin or harpoon thus constructed and fitted : the barbs are formed of bone, which are sharpened on the outer side, and hollowed within, for the purpose of forming a socket for the staff; these are then secured firmly together with a whale sinew, the point being fitted so as to receive a piece of mussel-shell, which is ground to a very sharp edge, and secured in its place by means of turpentine.[1] To this head or prong is fastened a strong line of whale sinew about nine feet in length, to the end of which is tied a bark rope from fifty to sixty fathoms long, having from twenty to thirty seal-skin floats or buoys attached to it at certain intervals, in order to check the motion of the whale and obstruct his diving. In the socket of the harpoon a staff or pole of about ten feet long, gradually tapering from

---

[1] The harpoon is at present a little different in construction. Pine resin, not "turpentine," is used for the purpose described, and the tips of deers' horns are utilised for the barbs. The most remarkable fact about the west coast of Vancouver Island whaling is its use of inflated seal-skins to impede the motion of the animal through the water. This is an Eskimo contrivance in use by the Alaskans and other extreme northern tribes, from whom the West Vancouverians seem to have borrowed it. In Sproat's *Scenes and Studies of Savage Life*, p. 226, there is an excellent description of whaling as practised in that part of Vancouver Island. The species pursued is usually finbacks, though a "black fish" with good whalebone is occasionally captured.

the middle to each end, is placed; this the harpooner holds in his hand, in order to strike the whale, and immediately detaches it as soon as the fish is struck.

The whale is considered as the king's fish, and no other person, when he is present, is permitted to touch him until the royal harpoon has first drawn his blood, however near he may approach; and it would be considered almost a sacrilege for any of the common people to strike a whale before he is killed, particularly if any of the chiefs should be present.[1] They also kill the porpoise[2] and sea-cow[3] with harpoons, but this inferior game is not interdicted the lower class.

With regard to their canoes, some of the handsomest

---

[1] The honour of using the harpoon is a hereditary privilege, enjoyed by only a few men in a tribe, and previous to the whaling season the crews have to practise all manner of ascetic practices in order to ensure good luck in the venture.

[2] This porpoise Dr. Gray considered, after examining a skull which I brought to the British Museum in 1866, to differ little, if at all, from the *Phocæna communis* of the Atlantic; but Dr. (afterwards Sir) W. H. Flower (*List of the Specimens of Cetacea*, etc., 1885, p. 16) seems to be of a different opinion.

[3] This "sea-cow," of which Meares also speaks as an animal hunted by the Nootka people, though rarely seen so far south, must, one might think, be another name for the seal or "sea-calf," were not the latter expressly referred to by name. The sea-cow, dugong, or manatee is not found in these seas, and the *Rhytina Stelleri*, once so abundant on Behring Island in Behring Strait, is generally considered to have been exterminated in the interval between 1741–1768. This, however, is hardly in accordance with fact, for, as evidence collected by Nordenskjöld proves, they were occasionally killed in 1780, while one was seen as late as 1854. It is therefore by no means improbable that in 1803 a few stragglers were still waiting their end on the shores of Vancouver Island. The sea-lion (*Eumetopias Stelleri*) is a seal also verging on extinction, the *Otaria ursinus* being now the fur seal of commerce (and politics) in that part of the North Pacific.

to be found on the whole coast are made at Nootka, though very fine ones are brought by the Wickinninish and the Kla-iz-zarts, who have them more highly ornamented. They are of all sizes, from such as are capable of holding only one person to their largest war canoes, which will carry forty men, and are extremely light. Of these, the largest of any that I ever saw was one belonging to Maquina, which I measured, and found to be forty-two feet six inches in length at the bottom, and forty - six feet from stem to stern. These are made of pine,[1] hollowed out from a tree with their chisels solely, which are about three inches broad and six in length, and set into a handle of very hard wood.

This instrument was formerly made of flint, or some hard stone ground down to as sharp an edge as possible, but since they have learned the use of iron, they have almost all of them of that metal. Instead of a mallet for striking this chisel, they make use of a smooth round stone, which they hold in the palm of the hand. With this same awkward instrument they not only excavate their canoes and trays and smooth their planks, but cut down such trees as they want, either for building, fuel, or other purposes, a labour which is mostly done by their slaves.

The felling of trees, as practised by them, is a slow and most tedious process, three of them being generally from two to three days in cutting down a large one; yet so attached were they to their own method, that notwithstanding they saw Thompson frequently, with one of our axes, of which there was a number saved, fell a

[1] A species of cedar (*Thuja*) is the wood used.

INDIAN CANOES, VICTORIA, V. I. (TEMP. 1863).

tree in less time than they could have gone round it
with their chisels, still they could not be persuaded to
make use of them.

After hollowing out their canoes, which they do very
neatly, they fashion the outside, and slightly burn it, for
the purpose of removing any splinters or small points
that might obstruct its passage through the water, after
which they rub it over thoroughly with rushes or coarse
mats, in order to smooth it, which not only renders it
almost as smooth as glass, but forms a better security
for it from the weather; this operation of burning and
rubbing down the bottoms of their canoes is practised
as often as they acquire any considerable degree of
roughness from use. The outside by this means
becomes quite black, and to complete their work they
paint the inside of a bright red, with ochre or some
other similar substance; the prows and sterns are almost
always ornamented with figures of ducks or some other
kind of bird, the former being so fashioned as to represent
the head, and the latter the tail; these are separate pieces
from the canoe, and are fastened to it with small flexible
twigs or bark cord.

Some of these canoes, particularly those employed in
whaling, which will hold about ten men, are ornamented
within about two inches below the gunwale with two
parallel lines on each side of very small white shells,
running fore and aft, which has a very pretty effect.
Their war canoes have no ornament of this kind, but
are painted on the outside with figures in white chalk,
representing eagles, whales, human heads, etc. They
are very dexterous in the use of their paddles, which are
very neatly wrought, and are five feet long, with a short

handle and a blade seven inches broad in the middle, tapering to a sharp point. With these they will make a canoe skim very swiftly on the water, with scarcely any noise, while they keep time to the stroke of the paddle with their songs.

CHAPTER VIII

MUSIC — MUSICAL   INSTRUMENTS — SLAVES — NEIGH-
BOURING TRIBES—TRADE WITH THESE—ARMY

THEY have a number which they sing on various occasions—as war,[1] whaling and fishing, at their marriages
and feasts, and at public festivals or solemnities. The
language of the most of these appears to be very
different in many respects from that used in their
common conversation, which leads me to believe either
that they have a different mode of expressing themselves in poetry, or that they borrow their songs from
their neighbours; and what the more particularly induces
me to the latter opinion is, that whenever any of the
Newchemass, a people from the northward, and who
speak a very different language, arrived, they used to
tell me that they expected a new song, and were almost
always sure to have one.

Their tunes are generally soft and plaintive, and
though not possessing great variety, are not deficient in
harmony. Their singing is generally accompanied with
several rude kinds of instrumental music, among the
most prominent of which is a kind of a drum. This is

[1] A specimen of one of their war-songs will be found at the end of this
work.

9

nothing more than a long plank hollowed out on the under side and made quite thin, which is beat upon by a stick of about a foot long, and renders a sound not unlike beating on the head of an empty cask, but much louder.

But the two most favourite instruments are the rattle and the pipe or whistle; these are, however, only used by the king, the chiefs, or some particular persons. The former is made of dried sealskin, so as to represent a fish, and is filled with a number of small smooth pebbles; it has a short handle, and is painted red. The whistle is made of bone, generally the leg of a deer; it is short, but emits a very shrill sound. They have likewise another kind of music, which they make use of in dancing, in the manner of castanets. This is produced by a number of mussel or cockle shells tied together and shaken to a kind of tune, which is accompanied with the voice.

Their slaves, as I have observed, form their most valuable species of property. These are of both sexes, being either captives taken by themselves in war, or purchased from the neighbouring tribes, and who reside in the same house, forming as it were a part of the family, are usually kindly treated, eat of the same food, and live as well as their masters. They are compelled, however, at times to labour severely, as not only all the menial offices are performed by them, such as bringing water, cutting wood, and a variety of others, but they are obliged to make the canoes, to assist in building and repairing the houses, to supply their masters with fish, and to attend them in war and to fight for them.

None but the king and chiefs have slaves, the common
people being prevented from holding them, either from
their inability to purchase them, or, as I am rather inclined to think, from its being considered as the privilege
of the former alone to have them,[1] especially as all those
made prisoners in war belong either to the king or the
chiefs who have captured them, each one holding such
as have been taken by himself or his slaves. There is
probably, however, some little distinction in favour of
the king, who is always the commander of the expedition, as Maquina had nearly fifty, male and female, in
his house, a number constituting about one half of its
inhabitants, comprehending those obtained by war and
purchase; whereas none of the other chiefs had more
than twelve. The females are employed principally in
manufacturing cloth, in cooking, collecting berries, etc.,
and with regard to food and living in general have not a
much harder lot than their mistresses, the principal differ-
ence consisting in these poor unfortunate creatures being
considered as free to any one, their masters prostituting
them whenever they think proper for the purpose of
gain. In this way many of them are brought on board
the ships and offered to the crews, from whence an
opinion appears to have been formed by some of our
navigators injurious to the chastity of their females,
than which nothing can be more generally untrue, as
perhaps in no part of the world is that virtue more
prized.[2]

The houses at Nootka, as already stated, are about

---

[1] This was not the case. Any free-born native, provided he had the
means, could own a slave.

[2] This is largely a tale of the past.

twenty, without comprising those inhabited by the Klahars, a small tribe that has been conquered and incorporated into that of Nootka, though they must be considered as in a state of vassalage, as they are not permitted to have any chiefs among them, and live by themselves in a cluster of small houses at a little distance from the village. The Nootka tribe, which consists of about five hundred warriors,[1] is not only more numerous than almost any of the neighbouring tribes, but far exceeds them in the strength and martial spirit of its people ; and in fact there are but few nations within a hundred miles either to the north or south but are considered as tributary to them.

In giving some account of the tribes that were accustomed to visit Nootka, I shall commence at the southward with the Kla-iz-zarts, and the Wickinninish, premising that in point of personal appearance there prevails a wonderful diversity between the various tribes on the coast, with the exception of the feet and legs, which are badly shaped in almost all of them from their practice of sitting on them.

The Kla-iz-zarts are a numerous and powerful tribe, living nearly three hundred miles to the south, and are said to consist of more than a thousand warriors.[2] They appear to be more civilised than any of the others, being better and more neatly dressed, more mild and affable in their manners, remarkable for their sprightliness and vivacity, and celebrated for their singing and dancing.

---

[1] It is questionable if there are now as many people in the whole tribe. Cook estimated the population of Friendly Cove at two thousand.

[2] This is wrong. The Kla-iz-zarts (Klahosahts) live *north* of Nootka Sound.

They exhibit also greater marks of improvement in whatever is wrought by them; their canoes, though not superior to those of Nootka in point of form and lightness, are more highly ornamented, and their weapons and tools of every kind have a much higher finish and display more skill in the workmanship. Their cast of countenance is very different from that of the Nootkians, their faces being very broad, with a less prominent nose and smaller eyes, and the top of the head flattened as if it had been pressed down with a weight. Their complexion is also much fairer, and their stature shorter, though they are well formed and strongly set.

They have a custom which appears to be peculiar to them, as I never observed it in any of the other tribes, which is to pluck out not only their beards and the hair from their bodies, but also their eyebrows, so as not to leave a vestige remaining. They were also in general more skilful in painting and decorating themselves, and I have seen some of them with no less than a dozen holes in each of their ears, to which were suspended strings of small beads about two inches in length. Their language is the same as spoken at Nootka, but their pronunciation is much more hoarse and guttural. These people are not only very expert in whaling, but are great hunters of the sea-otter and other animals, with which their country is said to abound, and the metamelth, a large animal of the deer kind, the skin of which I have already spoken of, another of a light grey colour, with very fine hair, from which they manufacture a handsome cloth, the beaver, and a species of large wild cat or tiger cat.

The Wickinninish,[1] their neighbours on the north, are about two hundred miles from Nootka. They are a robust, strong, and warlike people, but considered by the Nootkians as their inferiors in courage. This tribe is more numerous than that of Nootka, amounting to between six and seven hundred warriors. Though not so civilised as the Kla-iz-zarts, and less skilful in their manufactures, like them they employ themselves in hunting, as well as in whaling and fishing. Their faces are broad, but less so than the Kla-iz-zarts, with a darker complexion and a much less open and pleasing expression of countenance, while their heads present a very different form, being pressed in at the sides and lengthened towards the top somewhat in the shape of a sugar loaf. These people are very frequent visitors at Nootka, a close friendship subsisting between the two nations, Maquina's *Arcomah* or queen, *Y-ya-tintla-no*, being the daughter of the Wickinninish king.

The Kla-oo-quates[2] adjoining them on the north are much less numerous, their force not exceeding four hundred fighting men; they are also behind them in the arts of life. These are a fierce, bold, and enterprising people, and there were none that visited Nootka, whom Maquina used to be more on his guard against, or viewed

[1] In Meares's time (1788) Wickinninish was regarded as the most powerful chief, next to Maquina or Maquilla, as he calls him. His residence was usually at "Port Cox" (Clayoquat Sound), but his territory extended as far south as Nettinaht, his subjects comprising thirteen thousand people. Meares does not fall into Jewitt's blunder of confounding the name of the chief with that of his tribe. But Meares derived his information first hand, while Jewitt obtained it merely from hearsay, never having visited any other part except the immediate vicinity of Nootka Sound.

[2] Klayoquahts. They have now barely two hundred warriors.

with so much suspicion. The Eshquates[1] are about
the same number; these are considered as tributary
to Maquina. Their coast abounds with rivers, creeks,
and marshes.

UK-LULAC-AHT INDIAN.

To the north the nearest tribe of any importance is
the Aitizzarts;[2] these, however, do not exceed three

[1] Hishquahts. If they have twenty men, that is all. Thirty years ago
they had only thirty adult males.

[2] Ayhuttisahts. Thirty years ago they had thirty-six men fit to fight.

hundred warriors.   In appearance they greatly resemble the people of Nootka, to whom they are considered as tributary, their manners, dress, and style of living also being very similar.   They reside at about forty miles' distance up the Sound.   A considerable way farther to the northward are the Cayuquets; [1] these are a much more numerous tribe than that of Nootka, but thought by the latter to be deficient in courage and martial spirit, Maquina having frequently told me that their hearts were a little like those of birds.

There are also both at the north and south many other intervening tribes, but in general small in number and insignificant, all of whom, as well as the above-mentioned, speak the same language.   But the Newche-mass, who come from a great way to the northward, and from some distance inland, as I was told by Maquina, speak quite a different language,[2] although it is well understood by those of Nootka.   These were the most savage-looking and ugly men that I ever saw, their complexion being much darker, their stature shorter, and their hair coarser, than that of the other nations, and their dress and appearance dirty in an extreme. They wear their beards long like Jews, and have a very morose and surly countenance.   Their usual dress is a *kotsuk* made of wolf-skin, with a number of the tails attached to it, of which I have seen no less than ten on one garment, hanging from the top to the bottom;

---

[1] Ky-yoh-quahts.   In 1860 they numbered two hundred and thirty adult men.

[2] Namely, the Kwakiool spoken on the east and north coasts of Vancouver Island from Comox northwards.

though they sometimes wear a similar mantle of bark cloth, of a much coarser texture than that of Nootka, the original of which appears to be the same, though from their very great filthiness it was almost impossible to discover what it had been.

Their mode of dressing the hair also varies essentially from that of the other tribes, for they suffer that on the back of the head to hang loose, and bind the other over their foreheads in the manner of a fillet, with a strip of their country cloth, ornamented with small white shells. Their weapons are the *cheetolth*, or war-club, which is made from whalebone, daggers, bow and arrows, and a kind of spear pointed with bone or copper.[1] They brought with them no furs for sale, excepting a few wolf-skins, their merchandise consisting principally of the black shining mineral called *pelpelth*, and the fine red paint, which they carefully kept in close mat bags, some small dried salmon, clams, and roes of fish, with occasionally a little coarse matting cloth. They were accustomed to remain a much longer time at Nootka than the other tribes, in order to recover from the fatigue of a long journey, part of which was overland, and on these occasions taught their songs to our savages.

The trade of most of the other tribes with Nootka was principally train-oil, seal or whale's blubber, fish fresh or dried, herring or salmon spawn, clams and mussels, and the *yama*,[2] a species of fruit which is pressed and dried, cloth, sea-otter skins, and slaves.

---

[1] These implements have fallen out of use.

[2] The salal (*Gaultheria Shallon*), which forms a carpet to the ground, especially where the soil is poor.

From the Aitizzarts and the Cayuquets, particularly the former, the best Ife-whaw and in the greatest quantities was obtained. The Eshquates furnished us with wild ducks and geese, particularly the latter. The Wickinninish and Kla-iz-zarts brought to market many slaves, the best sea-otter skins, great quantities of oil, whale sinew, and cakes of the *yama*, highly ornamented canoes, some Ife-whaw, red ochre and pelpelth of an inferior quality to that obtajned from the Newchemass, but particularly the so much valued metamelth, and an excellent root called by the Kla-iz-zarts *Quawnoose.*[1] This is the size of a small onion, but rather longer, being of a tapering form like a pear, and of a brownish colour. It is cooked by steam, is always brought in baskets ready prepared for eating, and is in truth a very fine vegetable, being sweet, mealy, and of a most agreeable flavour. It was highly esteemed by the natives, who used to eat it, as they did .everything else, with train-oil. From the Kla-iz-zarts was also received, though in no great quantity, a cloth manufactured by them from the fur already spoken of, which feels like wool and is of a grey colour.

Many of the articles thus brought, particularly the provisions, were considered as presents, or tributary offerings, but this must be viewed as little more than a nominal acknowledgment of superiority, as they rarely failed to get the full amount of the value of their presents.

---

[1] The bulb of a pretty blue lily (*Gamassia esculenta*), well known all over North-West America as the "gamass" or "kamass." The digging and storing of it in summer form one of the most picturesque of Indian occupations. The gamass camps are always lively, and the skill and industry which a girl displays in this important part of her future duties are carefully noted by the young men in search of wives.

I have known eighteen of the great tubs, in which they keep their provisions, filled with spawn brought in this way. On these occasions a great feast is always made, to which not only the strangers, but the whole village, men, women, and children, are generally invited, and I have seen five of the largest tubs employed at such time, in cooking at the king's house. At these feasts they generally indulge in eating to an excess, making up in this respect for their want of inebriating liquors, which they know no method of preparing in any form, their only drink being water.

Whenever they came to visit or trade, it was their general custom to stop a few miles distant, under the lee of some bluff or rock, and rig themselves out in their best manner, by painting and dressing their heads. On their first coming on shore, they were invited to eat by the king, when they brought to him such articles as he wanted, after which the rest of the inhabitants were permitted to purchase, the strangers being careful to keep them in their canoes until sold, under strict guard to prevent their being stolen, the disposition of these people for thieving being so great, that it is necessary to keep a watchful eye upon them.

This was their usual mode of traffic, but whenever they wished to purchase any particular object, as, for instance, a certain slave, or some other thing of which they were very desirous, the canoe that came for this purpose would lie off a little distance from the shore, and a kind of ambassador or representative of the king or chief by whom it was sent, dressed in their best manner, and with his head covered with the white down, would rise, and, after making known the object of his

mission in a pompous speech, hold up specimens of such
articles as he was instructed to offer in payment, mentioning the number or quantity of each, when, if the
bargain was concluded, the exchange was immediately
made.

On their visits of friendship or traffic, the chiefs alone
used to sleep on shore ; this was generally at the house
of the king or the head chief, the others passing the
night on board of their canoes, which was done not
only for the preservation of their property, but because
they were not permitted to remain on shore, lest they
might excite some disturbance or commit depredations.

All these people generally go armed, the common
class wearing only a dagger suspended from their neck
behind, with a string of metamelth, and sometimes
thrust in their girdles.   The chiefs, in addition to the
dagger, carry the cheetolth, or war-club, suspended in
the same manner beneath their mantles; this, in the
hands of a strong man, is a powerful weapon, in the
management of which some of the older chiefs are very
dexterous.   It is made from the bone of a whale, and is
very heavy.   The blade is about eighteen inches long
and three broad, till it approaches near the point, where
it expands to the breadth of four inches.   In the middle,
from whence it slopes off gradually to an edge on each
side, it is from one to two inches in thickness.   This
blade is usually covered with figures of the sun and
moon, a man's head, etc.; and the hilt, which is made
to represent the head of a man or some animal, is
curiously set with small white shells, and has a band of
metamelth fastened to it, in order to sling it over the
shoulder.   Some of the tribes have also a kind of spear

headed with copper or the bone of the sting ray, which
is a dangerous weapon ; this is, however, not usual, and
only carried by the chiefs.   The bow and arrow are still
used by a few, but since the introduction of firearms
among them, this weapon has been mostly laid aside.

CHAPTER IX

SITUATION OF THE AUTHOR—REMOVAL TO TASHEES—
FISHING PARTIES

BUT to return to our unhappy situation. Though my
comrade and myself fared as well, and even better than
we could have expected among these people, considering
their customs and mode of living, yet our fears lest no
ship would come to our release, and that we should never
more behold a Christian country, were to us a source of
constant pain. Our principal consolation, in this gloomy
state, was to go on Sundays, whenever the weather
would permit, to the borders of a freshwater pond about
a mile from the village, where, after bathing and putting
on clean clothes, we would seat ourselves under the
shade of a beautiful pine, while I read some chapters in
the Bible, and the prayers appointed by our Church for
the day, ending our devotions with a fervent prayer to
the Almighty, that He would deign still to watch over
and preserve our lives, rescue us from the hands of the
savages, and permit us once more to behold a Christian
land.

In this manner were the greater part of our Sundays
passed at Nootka ; and I felt gratified to Heaven that,
amidst our other sufferings, we were at least allowed the

pleasure of offering up our devotions unmolested, for
Maquina, on my explaining to him as well as was in my
power the reason of our thus retiring at this time, far
from objecting, readily consented to it.

The pond above mentioned was small, not more
than a quarter of a mile in breadth, and of no great
length, the water being very clear, though not of great
depth, and bordered by a beautiful forest of pine, fir,
elm,[1] and beech,[1] free from bushes and underwood—a
most delightful retreat, which was rendered still more
attractive by a great number of birds that frequented
it, particularly the humming-bird.[2] Thither we used
to go to wash our clothes, and felt secure from any
intrusion from the natives, as they rarely visited it,
except for the purpose of cleansing themselves of their
paint.

In July we at length thought that the hope of delivery
we had so long anxiously indulged was on the point of
being gratified. A ship appeared in the offing; but,
alas! our fond hopes vanished almost as soon as formed ;
for, instead of standing in for the shore, she passed to
the northward, and soon disappeared. I shall not
attempt to describe our disappointment—my heart sank
within me, and I felt as though it was my destiny never
more to behold a Christian face. Four days after, there
occurred a tremendous storm of thunder and lightning,
during which the natives manifested great alarm and
terror, the whole tribe hurrying to Maquina's house,

---

[1] These trees are not found in Vancouver Island. Possibly, though
they are not very like, Jewitt mistook them for the Oregon alder and the
American ash, both trees of that locality.

[2] This is the migratory red-backed species (*Selasphorus rufus*, p. 19).

where, instead of keeping within, they seated themselves on the roof, amid the severest of the tempest, drumming upon the boards, and looking up to heaven, while the king beat the long hollow plank, singing, and, as he afterwards told me, begging *Quahootze,* the name they give to God, not to kill them, in which he was accompanied by the whole tribe; this singing and drumming was continued until the storm abated.

As the summer drew near its close, we began to suffer from the frequent want of food, which was principally owing to Maquina and the chiefs being out whaling, in which he would not permit Thompson and myself to join, lest we should make our escape to some of the neighbouring tribes. At these times the women seldom or ever cook any provision, and we were often hungry, but were sometimes fortunate enough to procure secretly a piece of salmon, some other fish, spawn, or even blubber, which, by boiling in salt water, with a few onions and turnips, the remains of the Spanish garden, or young nettles or other herbs, furnished us a delicious repast in private.

In the meantime, we frequently received accounts from the tribes who came to Nootka, both from the north and south, of there being vessels on the coast, and were advised by their chiefs to make our escape, who also promised us their aid, and to put us on board. These stories, however, as I afterwards learned, were almost all of them without any foundation, and merely invented by these people with a view to get us into their power, in order to make slaves of us themselves, or to sell us to others.

But I was still more strongly solicited to leave Nootka by a woman. This was a Wickinninish princess, a younger sister of Maquina's wife, who was there on a visit. I had the good fortune, if it may be so called, to become quite a favourite with her. She appeared much interested for me, asked me many questions respecting my country, if I had a mother and sister at home, and if they would not grieve for my absence. Her complexion was fairer than that of the women in general, and her features more regular, and she would have been quite handsome had it not been for a defect in one of her eyes, the sight of which had been injured by some accident; the reason, as Maquina told me, why she had not been married, a defect of this kind being by these savages considered as almost an insuperable objection. She urged me repeatedly to return with her, telling me that the Wickinninish were much better than the Nootkians; that her father would treat me more kindly than Maquina, give me better food and clothes, and finally put me on board one of my own country vessels. I felt, however, little disposed to accompany her, considering my situation with Maquina full as eligible as it would be with Wickinninish, if not better, notwithstanding all she said to the contrary.

On the 3rd of September the whole tribe quitted Nootka, according to their constant practice, in order to pass the autumn and winter at Tashees[1] and Cooptee, the latter lying about thirty miles up the Sound, in a deep bay, the navigation of which is very dangerous,

[1] "Tashis Canal" of seamen—the Tashis River flows in at its head. Coptee is at the mouth, Tashis farther up the stream.

10

from the great number of reefs and rocks with which it abounds.

On these occasions everything is taken with them, even the planks of their houses, in order to cover their new dwellings. To an European such a removal exhibits a scene quite novel and strange; canoes piled up with boards and boxes, and filled with men, women, and children, of all ranks and sizes, making the air resound with their cries and songs.

At these times, as well as when they have occasion to go some distance from their houses, the infants are usually suspended across the mother's shoulders, in a kind of cradle or hammock, formed of bark, of about six inches in depth, and of the length of the child, by means of a leather band inserted through loops on its edges; this they also keep them in when at home, in order to preserve them in a straight position, and prevent any distortion of the limbs, most probably a principal cause of these people being so seldom deformed or crooked.

The longboat of our ship having been repaired and furnished with a sail by Thompson, Maquina gave us the direction of it, we being better acquainted with managing it than his people, and, after loading her as deep as she could swim, we proceeded in company with them to the north, quitting Nootka with heavy hearts, as we could entertain no hopes of release until our return, no ships ever coming to that part of the coast. Passing Cooptee, which is situated on the southern bank, just within the mouth of a small river flowing from the east in a narrow valley at the foot of a mountain, we proceeded about fifteen miles up this stream to Tashees,

between a range of lofty hills on each side, which extend
a great distance inland, and are covered with the finest
forest trees of the country.   Immediately on our arrival,
we all went to work very diligently in covering the
houses with the planks we had brought, the frames
being ready erected, these people never pretending to
remove the timber.   In a very short time the work
was completed, and we were established in our new
residence.

Tashees is pleasantly situated, and in a most secure
position from the winter storms, in a small vale or
hollow on the south shore, at the foot of a mountain.
The spot on which it stands is level, and the soil very
fine, the country in its vicinity abounding with the most
romantic views, charmingly diversified, and fine streams
of water falling in beautiful cascades from the mountains.
The river at this place is about twenty rods in width,
and, in its deepest part, from nine to twelve feet.
This village is the extreme point of navigation, as,
immediately beyond, the river becomes much more
shallow, and is broken into falls and rapids.   The
houses here are placed in a line like those at Nootka,
but closer together, the situation being more confined;
they are also smaller, in consequence of which we were
much crowded, and incommoded for room.

The principal object in coming to this place is the
facility it affords these people of providing their winter
stock of provisions, which consists principally of salmon,
and the spawn of that fish; to which may be added
herrings and sprats, and herring spawn.   The latter,
however, is always procured by them at Nootka, previous
to their quitting it.   At the seasons of spawning, which

are early in spring and the last of August, they collect a great quantity of pine branches, which they place in different parts of the Cove at the depth of about ten feet, and secure them by means of heavy stones. On these the herring deposit their spawn in immense quantities; the bushes are then taken up, the spawn stripped from the branches, and, after being washed and freed from the pine leaves by the women, is dried and put up in baskets for use. It is considered as their greatest delicacy, and eaten both cooked and raw; in the former case, being boiled and eaten with train-oil, and in the latter, mixed up with cold water alone.

The salmon are taken at Tashees, principally in pots or wears. Their method of taking them in wears is thus :—A pot of twenty feet in length, and from four to five feet diameter at the mouth, is formed of a great number of pine splinters, which are strongly secured, an inch and a half from each other, by means of hoops made of flexible twigs, and placed about eight inches apart. At the end it tapers almost to a point, near which is a small wicker door for the purpose of taking out the fish. This pot or wear is placed at the foot of a fall or rapid, where the water is not very deep, and the fish, driven from above with long poles, are intercepted and caught in the wear, from whence they are taken into the canoes. In this manner I have seen more than seven hundred salmon caught in the space of fifteen minutes.[1] I have also sometimes

---

[1] Salmon used to be bought at Alberni at the rate of a cent apiece. There have been times when the garden at Fort Rupert was manured with fresh salmon,

SALMON WEAR NEAR THE INDIAN VILLAGE OF QUAMICHAN, V. I.

known a few of the striped bass taken in this manner, but rarely.

At such times there is great feasting and merriment among them. The women and female slaves being busily employed in cooking, or in curing the fish for their winter stock, which is done by cutting off the heads and tails, splitting them, taking out the back bone, and hanging them up in their houses to dry. They also dry the halibut and cod, but these, instead of curing whole, they cut up into small pieces for that purpose, and expose to the sun.

The spawn of the salmon, which is a principal article of their provision, they take out, and, without any other preparation, throw it into their tubs, where they leave it to stand and ferment, for, though they frequently eat it fresh, they esteem it much more when it has acquired a strong taste, and one of the greatest favours they can confer on any person, is to invite him to eat *Quakamiss,* the name they give this food, though scarcely anything can be more repugnant to an European palate, than it is in this state; and whenever they took it out of these large receptacles, which they are always careful to fill, such was the stench which it exhaled, on being moved, that it was almost impossible for me to abide it, even after habit had in a great degree dulled the delicacy of my senses. When boiled it became less offensive, though it still retained much of the putrid smell, and something of the taste.

Such is the immense quantity of these fish, and they are taken with such facility, that I have known upwards of twenty-five hundred brought into Maquina's house at once; and at one of their great feasts, have seen one hundred or more cooked in one of their largest tubs.

I used frequently to go out with Maquina upon these fishing parties, and was always sure to receive a handsome present of salmon, which I had the privilege of calling mine; I also went with him several times in a canoe, to strike the salmon, which I have attempted to do myself, but could never succeed, it requiring a degree of adroitness that I did not possess. I was also permitted to go out with a gun, and was several times very successful in shooting wild ducks and teal, which are very numerous here, though rather shy. These they cooked in their usual manner, by boiling, without any farther dressing than skinning them.

In many respects, however, our situation was less pleasant here than at Nootka. We were more incommoded for room, the houses not being so spacious, nor so well arranged, and as it was colder, we were compelled to be much more within doors. We, however, did not neglect on Sundays, when the weather would admit, to retire into the woods, and, by the side of some stream, after bathing, return our thanks to God for preserving us, and offer up to Him our customary devotions.

I was, however, very apprehensive, soon after our arrival at this place, that I should be deprived of the satisfaction of keeping my journal, as Maquina one day, observing me writing, inquired of me what I was doing, and when I endeavoured to explain it, by telling him that I was keeping an account of the weather, he said it was not so, and that I was speaking bad about him, and telling how he had taken our ship and killed the crew, ·so as to inform my countrymen, and that if he ever saw me writing in it again, he would throw it into the fire. I was much rejoiced that he did no more than threaten, and became very cautious afterwards not to let him see me write.

Not long after, I finished some daggers for him, which I polished highly ; these pleased him much, and he gave me directions to make a cheetolth, in which I succeeded so far to his satisfaction, that he gave me a present of cloth sufficient to make me a complete suit of raiment, besides other things.

Thompson also, who had become rather more of a favourite than formerly, since he had made a fine sail for his canoe, and some garments for him out of European cloth, about this time completed another, which was thought by the savages a most superb dress. This was a *kotsuk* or mantle, a fathom square, made entirely of European vest patterns of the gayest colours. These were sewed together in a manner to make the best show, and bound with a deep trimming of the finest otterskin, with which the arm-holes were also bordered ; while the bottom was further embellished with five or six rows of gilt buttons, placed as near as possible to each other.

Nothing could exceed the pride of Maquina when he first put on this royal robe, decorated, like the coat of Joseph, with all the colours of the rainbow, and glittering with the buttons, which as he strutted about made a tinkling, while he repeatedly exclaimed, in a transport of exultation, "*Klew shish Kotsuk—wick kum atack Nootka.*"[1]—" A fine garment—Nootka can't make them."

Maquina, who knew that the chiefs of the tribes who came to visit us had endeavoured to persuade me to escape, frequently cautioned me not to listen to them, saying that, should I make the attempt, and he were to take me, he should certainly put me to death. While here, he gave me a book, in which I found the names of seven persons belonging to the ship *Manchester*, of Philadelphia, Captain Brian—viz. Daniel Smith, Lewis Gillon, James Tom, Clark, Johnson, Ben, and Jack. These men, as Maquina informed me, ran away from the ship and came to him, but that six of them soon after went off in the night, with an intention to go to the Wickinninish, but were stopped by the Eshquates, and sent back to him, and that he ordered them to be put to death ; and a most cruel death it was, as I was told by one of the natives, four men holding one of them on the ground, and forcing open his mouth, while they choked him by ramming stones down his throat.

As to Jack, the boy, who made no attempt to go off, Maquina afterwards sold him to the Wickinninish. I was informed by the Princess Yuqua that he was quite a small boy, who cried a great deal, being put to hard labour beyond his strength by the natives, in cutting

---

[1] This is a fair specimen of the kind of *lingua franca* which even then had begun to spring up in the intercourse of the early traders with the Indians, and which by now takes the shape of the Chinook Jargon. For, apart from the imperfectly pronounced Indian words, there is no such term as Nootka in any language. It was a misconception of the first visitors there. They probably mistook *Nootchee*, a mountain, for the name of the country generally (p. 29).

wood and bringing water, and that when he heard of the murder of our crew, it had such an effect on him, that he fell sick, and died shortly after. On learning the melancholy fate of this unfortunate lad, it again awakened in my bosom those feelings that I had experienced at the shocking death of my poor comrades.

CHAPTER X

CONVERSATION WITH MAQUINA—FRUITS—RELIGIOUS CEREMONIES—VISIT TO UPQUESTA

THE king, finding that I was desirous of learning their language, was much delighted, and took great pleasure in conversing with me. On one of these occasions he explained to me his reasons for cutting off our ship, saying that he bore no ill will to my countrymen, but that he had been several times treated very ill by them. The first injury of which he had cause to complain, was done him by a Captain Tawnington, who commanded a schooner which passed a winter at Friendly Cove, where he was well treated by the inhabitants. This man, taking advantage of Maquina's absence, who had gone to the Wickinninish to procure a wife, armed himself and crew, and entered the house, where there were none but women, whom he threw into the greatest consternation, and, searching the chests, took away all the skins, of which Maquina had no less than forty of the best; and that about the same time, four of their chiefs were barbarously killed by a Captain Martinez, a Spaniard.[1]

---

[1] This was probably Don Estevan Martinez, who, on the 6th of May 1789, arrived in the corvette *Princesa*, to take possession of the country for his sovereign. He it was who landed materials and artillery, and began to erect a fort on a small island at the entrance to Friendly Cove. He seems

That soon after, Captain Hanna, of the *Sea Otter*,[1] in consequence of one of the natives having stolen a chisel from the carpenter, fired upon their canoes which were alongside, and killed upwards of twenty of the natives, of whom several were *Tyees* or chiefs; and that he himself, being on board the vessel, in order to escape was obliged to leap from the quarter-deck, and swim for a long way under water.

These injuries had excited in the breast of Maquina an ardent desire of revenge, the strongest passion of the savage heart, and though many years had elapsed since their commission, still they were not forgotten, and the want of a favourable opportunity alone prevented him from sooner avenging them. Unfortunately for us, the long-wished-for opportunity at length presented itself in

to have been a most high-handed kind of Don, for he seized the British vessels *Iphigenia, North-West America, Argonaut,* and *Princess Royal,* then trading under the Portuguese flag, and acted in so arbitrary a manner to the officers and crew, that it was easy to believe he was not over scrupulous in his dealings with the Indians. It was during his stay in Nootka Sound that Callicum, a relation of Maquina's, and next to him in rank, was barbarously murdered by an officer on board one of the Spanish ships, and his father refused permission to dive for the body until he had handed over a number of skins to the white savage.

[1] Captain James Hanna was the second European to enter Nootka Sound after Captain Cook had left it. The *Sea Otter*, a vessel under 70 tons, was fitted out in China, and reached Nootka in August 1785; when Maquina, presuming upon the inferior size of the craft and the small number of the crew, made a desperate attack upon her. This was repulsed by the courage of the ship's company, after which business proceeded on such friendly terms that he procured five hundred and eighty-five sea-otter skins in five weeks, which were sold in Canton for 20,600 dollars. It was Hanna who discovered Fitzhugh Sound, Lance Island, Sea Otter Harbour, and other now well-known spots on the North-West coast of America. The incident related by Maquina is not to be found in the records of the expedition which have descended to us. He made another voyage in 1786, solely for commercial purposes.

our ship, which Maquina finding not guarded with the usual vigilance of the North-West traders, and feeling his desire of revenge rekindled by the insult offered him by Captain Salter, formed a plan for attacking, and on his return called a council of his chiefs, and communicated it to them, acquainting them with the manner in which he had been treated. No less desirous of avenging this affront offered their king than their former injuries, they readily agreed to his proposal, which was to go on board without arms as usual, but under different pretexts, in great numbers, and wait for his signal for the moment of attacking their unsuspecting victims. The execution of this scheme, as the reader knows, was unhappily too successful.

And here I cannot but indulge a reflection that has frequently occurred to me on the manner in which our people behave towards the natives. For, though they are a thievish race, yet I have no doubt that many of the melancholy disasters have principally arisen from the imprudent conduct of some of the captains and crews of the ships employed in this trade, in exasperating them by insulting, plundering, and even killing them on slight grounds. This, as nothing is more sacred with a savage than the principle of revenge, and no people are so impatient under insult, induces them to wreak their vengeance upon the first vessel or boat's crew that offers, making the innocent too frequently suffer for the wrongs of the guilty, as few of them know how to discriminate between persons of the same general appearance, more especially when speaking the same language. And to this cause do I believe must principally be ascribed the sanguinary disposition with

CALLICUM AND MAQUILLA, CHIEFS OF NOOTKA SOUND.

which these people are reproached, as Maquina repeatedly told me that it was not his wish to hurt a white man, and that he never should have done it, though ever so much in his power, had they not injured him.

And were the commanders of our ships to treat the savages with rather more civility than they sometimes do, I am inclined to think they would find their account in it ; not that I should recommend to them a confidence in the good faith and friendly professions of these people, so as in any degree to remit their vigilance, but, on the contrary, to be strictly on their guard, and suffer but a very few of them to come on board the ship, and admit not many of their canoes alongside at a time ; a precaution that would have been the means of preventing some of the unfortunate events that have occurred, and if attended to, may in future preserve many a valuable life.   Such a regulation, too, from what I know of their disposition and wants, would produce no serious difficulty in trading with the savages, and they would soon become perfectly reconciled to it.

Among the provisions which the Indians procure at Tashees, I must not omit mentioning a fruit that is very important, as forming a great article of their food.   This is what is called by them the *Yama*,[1] a species of berry that grows in bunches like currants, upon a bush from two to three feet high, with a large, round, and smooth leaf.   This berry is black, and about the size of a pistol shot, but of rather an oblong shape, and open at the top like the blue whortleberry.   The taste is sweet, but a little acrid, and when first gathered, if eaten in any great

[1] *Gaultheria Shallon* (see p. 137).

quantity, especially without oil, is apt to produce colics. To procure it, large companies of women go out on the mountains, accompanied by armed men to protect them against wild beasts, where they frequently remain for several days, kindling a fire at night, and sheltering themselves under sheds constructed of boughs. At these parties they collect great quantities. I have known Maquina's queen and her women return loaded, bringing with them upwards of twelve bushels. In order to preserve it, it is pressed in the bunches between two planks, and dried and put away in baskets for use. It is always eaten with oil.

Of berries of various kinds, such as strawberries, raspberries, blackberries, etc., there are great quantities in the country, of which the natives are very fond, gathering them in their seasons, and eating them with oil, but the yama is the only one that they preserve.

Fish is, however, their great article of food, as almost all the others, excepting the yama, may be considered as accidental. They nevertheless are far from dis-relishing meat, for instance, venison and bear's flesh. With regard to the latter, they have a most singular custom, which is, that any one who eats of it is obliged to abstain from eating any kind of fresh fish whatever for the term of two months, as they have a superstitious belief that, should any of their people, after tasting bear's flesh, eat of fresh salmon, cod, etc., the fish, though at ever so great a distance off, would come to the know-ledge of it, and be so much offended thereat as not to allow themselves to be taken by any of the inhabit-ants. This I had an opportunity of observing while at Tashees, a bear having been killed early in December, of which not more than ten of the natives would eat, being prevented by the prohibition annexed to it, which also was the reason of my comrade and myself not tasting it, on being told by Maquina the consequences.

As there is something quite curious in their management of this animal, when they have killed one, I shall give a description of it. After well cleansing the bear from the dirt and blood with which it is generally covered when killed, it is brought in and seated opposite the king in an upright posture, with a chief's bonnet, wrought in figures, on its head, and its fur powdered over with the white down. A tray of provision is then set before it, and it is invited by words and gestures to eat. This mock ceremony over, the reason of which I could never learn, the animal is taken and skinned, and the flesh and entrails boiled up into a soup, no part but the paunch being rejected.[1]

This dressing the bear, as they call it, is an occasion of great rejoicing throughout the village, all the inhabitants being invited to a great feast at the king's house, though but few of them, in consequence of the penalty, will venture to eat of the flesh, but generally content themselves with their favourite dish of herring spawn and water. The feast on this occasion was closed by a dance from Sat-sat-sok-sis, in the manner I have already described, in the course of which he repeatedly shifted his mask for another of a different form.

[1] These observances are well worth noting in connection with the others which attach to the bear among nearly all savage races.

A few days after, a second bear was taken, like the former, by means of a trap. This I had the curiosity to go and see at the place where it was caught, which was in the following manner:—On the edge of a small stream of water in the mountains which the salmon ascend, and near the spot where the bear is accustomed to watch for them, which is known by its track, a trap or box about the height of a man's head is built of posts and planks with a flat top, on which are laid a number of large stones or rocks. The top and sides are then carefully covered with turf, so as to resemble a little mound, and wholly to exclude the light, a narrow entrance of the height of the building only being left, just sufficient to admit the head and shoulders of the beast. On the inside, to a large plank that covers the top is suspended by a strong cord a salmon, the plank being left loose, so that a forcible pull will bring it down. On coming to its usual haunt, the bear enters the trap, and, in endeavouring to pull away the fish, brings down the whole covering with its load of stones upon its head, and is almost always crushed to death on the spot, or so wounded as to be unable to escape.[1]

They are always careful to examine these traps every day, in order, if a bear be caught, to bring it immediately, for it is not a little singular that these people will eat no kind of meat that is in the least tainted, or not perfectly fresh, while, on the contrary, it is hardly possible for fish to be in too putrid a state for them, and I have frequently known them, when a whale has been driven ashore, bring pieces of it home with them in a state of offensiveness insupportable to anything but a

---

[1] These traps are still in common use.

crow, and devour it with high relish, considering it as preferable to that which is fresh.

On the morning of the 13th of December, commenced what to us appeared a most singular farce. Apparently without any previous notice, Maquina discharged a pistol close to his son's ear, who immediately fell down as if killed, upon which all the women of the house set up a most lamentable cry, tearing handfuls of hair from their heads, and exclaiming that the prince was dead. At the same time a great number of the inhabitants rushed into the house, armed with their daggers, muskets, etc., inquiring the cause of their outcry. These were immediately followed by two others dressed in wolf-skins, with masks over their faces representing the head of that animal; the latter came in on their hands and feet in the manner of a beast, and, taking up the prince, carried him off upon their backs, retiring in the same manner they entered. We saw nothing more of the ceremony, as Maquina came to us, and, giving us a quantity of dried provision, ordered us to quit the house, and not return to the village before the expiration of seven days, for that if we appeared within that period, he should kill us.

At any other season of the year such an order would by us have been considered as an indulgence, in enabling us to pass our time in whatever way we wished; and even now, furnished as we were with sufficient provision for that term, it was not very unpleasant to us, more particularly Thompson, who was always desirous to keep as much as possible out of the society and sight of the natives, whom he detested. Taking with us our provisions, a bundle of clothes, and our axes, we obeyed the directions of Maquina, and withdrew into the woods, where we built ourselves a cabin to shelter us, with the branches of trees, and, keeping up a good fire, secured ourselves pretty well from the cold. Here we passed the prescribed period of our exile, with more content than much of the time while with them, employing the day in reading and praying for our release, or in rambling around and exploring the country, the soil of which we found to be very good, and the face of it, beautifully diversified with hills and valleys, refreshed with the finest streams of water, and at night enjoyed comfortable repose upon a bed of soft leaves, with our garments spread over us to protect us from the cold.

At the end of seven days we returned, and found several of the people of Ai-tiz-zart with their king or chief at Tashees, who had been invited by Maquina to attend the close of this performance, which I now learned was a celebration, held by them annually, in honour of their god, whom they call *Quahootze*,[1] to return him their thanks for his past, and implore his future favours. It terminated on the 21st, the day after our return, with a most extraordinary exhibition. Three men, each of whom had two bayonets run through his sides, between the ribs, apparently regardless of the pain, traversed the room, backwards and forwards, singing war-songs, and exulting in this display of firmness.

On the arrival of the 25th, we could not but call to mind that this, being Christmas, was in our country a day of the greatest festivity, when our fellow-countrymen, assembled in their churches, were celebrating the goodness of God and the praises of the Saviour. What a

---

[1] *Quawteaht*, the supreme being of all the tribes speaking the "Aht" language.

reverse did our situation offer!—captives in a savage land, and slaves to a set of ignorant beings, unacquainted with religion or humanity, hardly were we permitted to offer up our devotions by ourselves in the woods, while we felt even grateful for this privilege. Thither, with the king's permission, we withdrew, and, after reading the service appointed for the day, sung the hymn of the Nativity, fervently praying that Heaven in its goodness would permit us to celebrate the next festival of this kind in some Christian land.

On our return, in order to conform as much as was in our power to the custom of our country, we were desirous of having a better supper than usual. With this view, we bought from one of the natives some dried clams and oil, and a root called *Kletsup*,[1] which we cooked by steaming, and found it very palatable. This root consists of many fibres, of about six inches long, and of the size of a crow quill. It is sweet, of an agreeable taste, not unlike the *Quawnoose*, and it is eaten with oil. The plant that produces it I have never seen.

On the 31st all the tribe quitted Tashees for Cooptee, whither they go to pass the remainder of the winter, and complete their fishing, taking off everything with them in the same manner as at Nootka. We arrived in a few hours at Cooptee, which is about fifteen miles, and immediately set about covering the houses, which was soon completed.

This place, which is their great herring and sprat fishery, stands just within the mouth of the river, on the same side with Tashees, in a very narrow valley at the

This seems the bracken fern root, which is eaten. But the name usually applied to it is *Sheetla.*

foot of a high mountain. Though nearly as secure as Tashees from the winter storms, it is by no means so pleasantly situated, though to us it was a much more agreeable residence, as it brought us nearer Nootka, where we were impatient to return, in hopes of finding some vessel there, or hearing of the arrival of one near.

The first snow that fell this season was the day after our arrival, on New Year's Day; a day that, like Christmas, brought with it painful recollections, but at the same time led us to indulge the hope of a more fortunate year than the last.

Early on the morning of the 7th of January, Maquina took me with him in his canoe on a visit to Upquesta, chief of the Ai-tiz-zarts, who had invited him to attend an exhibition at his village, similar to the one with which he had been entertained at Tashees. This place is between twenty and thirty miles distant up the Sound, and stands on the banks of a small river about the size of that of Cooptee, just within its entrance, in a valley of much greater extent than that of Tashees; it consists of fourteen or fifteen houses, built and disposed in the manner of those at Nootka. The tribe, which is considered as tributary to Maquina, amounts to about three hundred warriors, and the inhabitants, both men and women, are among the best-looking of any people on the coast.

On our arrival we were received at the shore by the inhabitants, a few of whom were armed with muskets, which they fired, with loud shouts and exclamations of *Wocash, wocash!*

We were welcomed by the chief's messenger, or master

of ceremonies, dressed in his best garments, with his hair powdered with white down, and holding in his hand the cheetolth, the badge. of his office. This man preceded us to the chief's house, where he introduced and pointed out to us our respective seats. On ˏentering, the visitors took off their hats, which they always wear on similar occasions, and Maquina his outer robes, of which he has several on whenever he pays a visit, and seated himself near the chief.

As I was dressed in European clothes, I became quite an object of curiosity to these people, very few of whom had ever seen a white man. They crowded around me in numbers, taking hold of my clothes, examining my face, hands, and feet, and even opening my mouth to see if I had a tongue, for, notwithstanding I had by this time become well acquainted with their language, I preserved the strictest silence, Maquina on our first landing having enjoined me not to speak until he should direct.

Having undergone this examination for some time, Maquina at length made a sign to me to speak to them. On hearing me address them in their own language, they were greatly astonished and delighted, and told Maquina that they now perceived that I was a man like themselves, except that I was white, and looked like a seal, alluding to my blue jacket and trousers, which they wanted to persuade me to take off, as they did not like their appearance. Maquina in the meantime gave an account to the chief of the scheme he had formed for surprising our ship, and the manner in which he and his people had carried it into execution, with such particular and horrid details of that transaction as chilled the blood in my veins. Trays of boiled herring spawn and train-oil were soon after brought in and placed before us, neither the chief or any of his people eating at the same time, it being contrary to the ideas of hospitality entertained by these nations, to eat any part of the food that is provided for strangers, always waiting until their visitors have finished, before they have their own brought in.

The following day closed their festival with an exhibition of a similar kind to that which had been given at Tashees, but still more cruel; the different tribes appearing on these occasions to endeavour to surpass each other in their proofs of fortitude and endurance of pain. In the morning, twenty men entered the chief's house, with each an arrow run through the flesh of his sides and either arm, with a cord fastened to the end, which, as the performers advanced, singing and boasting, was forcibly drawn back by a person having hold of it. After this performance was closed, we returned to Cooptee, which we reached at midnight, our men keeping time with their songs to the stroke of their paddles.

The natives now began to take the herring and sprat in immense quantities, with some salmon, and there was nothing but feasting from morning till night.

The following is the method they employ to take the herring. A stick of about seven feet long, two inches broad, and half an inch thick, is formed from some hard wood, one side of which is set with sharp teeth, made from whalebone, at about half an inch apart. Provided with this instrument, the fisherman seats himself in the prow of a canoe, which is paddled by another, and whenever he comes to a shoal of herrings, which cover the water in great quantities, he strikes it with both hands upon them, and at the same moment, turning it up, brings it over the side of the canoe, into which he lets those that are taken drop. It is astonishing to see how many are caught by those who are dexterous at this kind of fishing, as they seldom fail, when the shoals are numerous, of taking as many as ten or twelve at a stroke, and in a very short time will fill a canoe with them. Sprats are likewise caught in a similar manner.

CHAPTER XI

RETURN TO NOOTKA (FRIENDLY COVE)—DEATH OF
MAQUINA'S NEPHEW—INSANITY OF TOOTOOSCH
—AN INDIAN MOUNTEBANK

ABOUT the beginning of February, Maquina gave a
great feast, at which were present not only all the
inhabitants, but one hundred persons from Ai-tiz-zart,
and a number from Wickinninish who had been invited
to attend it. It is customary with them to give an
annual entertainment of this kind, and it is astonishing
to see what a quantity of provision is expended, or
rather wasted, on such an occasion, when they always eat
to the greatest excess. It was at this feast that I saw
upwards of an hundred salmon cooked in one tub.
The whole residence at Cooptee presents an almost
uninterrupted succession of feasting and gormand-
ising, and it would seem as if the principal object
of these people was to consume their whole stock
of provision before leaving it, trusting entirely to
their success in fishing and whaling, for a supply at
Nootka.

On the 25th of February we quitted Cooptee, and
returned to Nootka. With much joy did Thompson
and myself again find ourselves in a place where, not-

withstanding the melancholy recollections which it excited, we hoped before long to see some vessel arrive to our relief, and for this we became the more solicitous, as of late we had become much more apprehensive of our safety, in consequence of information brought Maquina a few days before we left Cooptee, by some of the Cayuquets, that there were twenty ships at the northward, preparing to come against him, with an intent of destroying him and his whole tribe, for cutting off the *Boston.*

This story, which was wholly without foundation, and discovered afterwards to have been invented by these people, for the purpose of disquieting him, threw him into great alarm, and, notwithstanding all I could say to convince him that it was an unfounded report, so great was his jealousy of us, especially after it had been confirmed to him by some others of the same nation, that he treated us with much harshness, and kept a very suspicious eye upon us.

Nothing, indeed, could be more unpleasant than our present situation, when I reflected that our lives were altogether dependent on the will of a savage, on whose caprice and suspicions no rational calculation could be made.

Not long after our return, a son of Maquina's sister, a boy of eleven years old, who had been for some time declining, died. Immediately on his death, which was about midnight, all the men and women in the house set up loud cries and shrieks, which, awakening Thompson and myself, so disturbed us that we left the house. This lamentation was kept up during the remainder of the night. In the morning, a great fire was kindled, in which Maquina burned, in honour of the deceased, ten fathoms of cloth, and buried with him ten fathoms more, eight of Ife-whaw, four prime sea-otter skins, and two small trunks, containing our unfortunate captain's clothes and watch.

This boy was considered as a Tyee, or chief, being the only son of Tootoosch, one of their principal chiefs, who had married Maquina's sister, whence arose this ceremony on his interment: it being an established custom with these people, that whenever a chief dies, his most valuable property is burned or buried with him; it is, however, wholly confined to the chiefs, and appears to be a mark of honour appropriate to them.[1]   In this instance, Maquina furnished the articles, in order that his nephew might have the proper honours rendered him.

Tootoosch, his father, was esteemed the first warrior of the tribe, and was one who had been particularly active in the destruction of our ship, having killed two of

---

[1] When an Indian dies, all of his property which has not been given away, is either buried with him, or, in extreme cases, burned, not for the purpose of accompanying him to the Spirit Land, but, so the people have told me, to prevent any temptation to indulge in the bad luck of mentioning his name.   The only things that are exempted from this practice are the dead man's best canoes, his house-planks, and fishing and hunting implements, which, with any slaves he may possess, go to his eldest son. I have known the deceased's house and all its contents to be burned; but when this is not the case, then the materials are removed elsewhere, and another building is erected.   Around his grave—a box raised from the ground on pillars, often quaintly carved, or a canoe, or a box fixed up a tree—are placed various articles belonging to him (or her).   At one time they buried his money with him.   But for obvious reasons this custom has fallen into abeyance.

our poor comrades, who were ashore, whose names were Hall and Wood. About the time of our removal to Tashees, while in the enjoyment of the highest health, he was suddenly seized with a fit of delirium, in which he fancied that he saw the ghosts of those two men constantly standing by him, and threatening him, so that he would take no food, except what was forced into his mouth.

A short time before this he had lost a daughter of about fifteen years of age, which afflicted him greatly, and whether his insanity, a disorder very uncommon amongst these savages, no instance of the kind having occurred within the memory of the oldest man amongst them, proceeded from this cause, or that it was the special interposition of an all-merciful God in our favour, who by this means thought proper to induce these barbarians still further to respect our lives, or that, for hidden purposes, the Supreme Disposer of events sometimes permits the spirits of the dead to revisit the world, and haunt the murderer, I know not, but his mind, from this period until his death, which took place but a few weeks after that of his son, was incessantly occupied with the images of the men whom he had killed.

This circumstance made much impression upon the tribe, particularly the chiefs, whose uniform opposition to putting us to death, at the various councils that were held on our account, I could not but in part attribute to this cause; and Maquina used frequently, in speaking of Tootoosch's sickness, to express much satisfaction that his hands had not been stained with the blood of any of our men.

When Maquina was first informed by his sister of the strange conduct of her husband, he immediately went to his house, taking us with him; suspecting that his disease had been caused by us, and that the ghosts of our countrymen had been called thither by us, to torment him. We found him raving about Hall and Wood, saying that they were *peshak*, that is, bad.

Maquina then placed some provision before him, to see if he would eat. On perceiving it, he put forth his hand to take some, but instantly withdrew it with signs of horror, saying that Hall and Wood were there, and would not let him eat. Maquina then, pointing to us, asked if it was not John and Thompson who troubled him.

"*Wik*,"[1] he replied,—that is, no; "*John klushish—Thompson klushish*"—John and Thompson are both good; then, turning to me, and patting me on the shoulder, he made signs to me to eat. I tried to persuade him that Hall and Wood were not there, and that none were near him but ourselves; he said, " I know very well you do not see them, but I do."

At first Maquina endeavoured to convince him that he saw nothing, and to laugh him out of his belief, but, finding that all was to no purpose, he at length became serious, and asked me if I had ever seen anyone affected in this manner, and what was the matter with him. I gave him to understand, pointing to his head, that his brain was injured, and that he did not see things as formerly.

Being convinced by Tootoosch's conduct that we had

---

[1] *Wik* actually means "Not I." Good is *Klooceahatli* or *Klootakloosch.*

no agency in his indisposition, on our return home
Maquina asked me what was done in my country in
similar cases.

I told him that such persons were closely confined,
and sometimes tied up and whipped, in order to make
them better.[1]

After pondering for some time, he said that he
should be glad to do anything to relieve him, and that
he should be whipped, and immediately gave orders
to some of his men to go to Tootoosch's house, bind
him, and bring him to his, in order to undergo the
operation.

Thompson was the person selected to administer
this remedy, which he undertook very readily, and
for that purpose provided himself with a good number
of spruce branches, with which he whipped him most
severely, laying it on with the best will imaginable,
while Tootoosch displayed the greatest rage, kicking,
spitting, and attempting to bite all who came near
him. This was too much for Maquina, who at length,
unable to endure it longer, ordered Thompson to desist
and Tootoosch to be carried back, saying that if there
was no other way of curing him but by whipping, he
must remain mad.

The application of the whip produced no beneficial
effect on Tootoosch, for he afterwards became still more
deranged; in his fits of fury sometimes seizing a club

---

[1] This, it must be remembered, was in the days before Connolly.
Maquina's remark that if an insane man could not be cured but by
whipping him, he must remain mad, proves that the savage chief was
in advance of his time. Insanity is, however, extremely rare among the
Indians.

12

and beating his slaves in a most dreadful manner, and striking and spitting at all who came near him, till at length his wife, no longer daring to remain in the house with him, came with her son to Maquina's.

The whaling season now commenced, and Maquina was out almost every day in his canoe in pursuit of them, but for a considerable time with no success, one day breaking the staff of his harpoon, another after having been a long time fast to a whale, the weapon drawing, owing to the breaking of the shell which formed its point, with several such like accidents, arising from the imperfection of the instrument.

At these times he always returned very morose and out of temper, upbraiding his men with having violated their obligation to continence preparatory to whaling. In this state of ill-humour he would give us very little to eat, which, added to the women not cooking when the men are away, reduced us to a very low fare.

In consequence of the repeated occurrence of similar accidents, I proposed to Maquina to make him a harpoon or foreganger of steel, which would be less liable to fail him. The idea pleased him, and in a short time I completed one for him, with which he was much delighted, and the very next day went out to make a trial of it.

He succeeded with it in taking a whale. Great was the joy throughout the village as soon as it was known that the king had secured the whale, by notice from a person stationed at the headland in the offing. All the canoes were immediately launched, and, furnished with harpoons

and sealskin floats, hastened to assist in buoying it up
and towing it in.

The bringing in of this fish exhibited a scene of
universal festivity. As soon as the canoes appeared at
the mouth of the Cove, those on board of them singing
a triumph to a slow air, to which they kept time with
their paddles, all who were on shore, men, women, and
children, mounted the roofs of their houses to congratulate the king on his success, drumming most
furiously on the planks, and exclaiming *Wocash—wocash,
Tyee!*

The whale, on being drawn on shore, was immediately
cut up, and a great feast of the blubber given at
Maquina's house, to which all the village were invited,
who indemnified themselves for their Lent by eating as
usual to excess. I was highly praised for the goodness
of my harpoon, and a quantity of blubber given me,
which I was permitted to cook as I pleased ; this I boiled
in salt water with some young nettles and other greens
for Thompson and myself, and in this way we found it
tolerable food.

Their method of procuring the oil, is to skim it from
the water in which the blubber is boiled, and when cool,
put it up into whale bladders for use; and of these
I have seen them so large as, when filled, would require
no less than five or six men to carry. Several of the
chiefs, among whom were Maquina's brothers, who,
after the king has caught the first whale, are privileged
to take them also, were very desirous, on discovering
the superiority of my harpoon, that I should make
some for them, but this Maquina would not permit,
reserving for himself this improved weapon. He, how-

ever, gave me directions to make a number more for himself, which I executed, and also made him several lances, with which he was greatly pleased.

As these people have some very singular observances preparatory to whaling, an account of them will, I presume, not prove uninteresting, especially as it may serve to give a better idea of their manners. A short time before leaving Tashees, the king makes a point of passing a day alone on the mountain, whither he goes very privately early in the morning, and does not return till late in the evening.[1] This is done, as I afterwards learned, for the purpose of singing and praying to his God for success in whaling the ensuing season. At Cooptee the same ceremony is performed, and at Nootka after the return thither, with still greater solemnity, as for the next two days he appears very thoughtful and gloomy, scarcely speaking to any one, and observes a most rigid fast. On these occasions he has always a broad red fillet made of bark bound around his head, in token of humiliation, with a large branch of green spruce on the top, and his great rattle in his hand.

In addition to this, for a week before commencing their whaling, both himself and the crew of his canoe observe a fast, eating but very little, and going into the water several times in the course of each day to bathe, singing and rubbing their bodies, limbs, and faces with shells and bushes, so that on their return I have seen them look as though they had been severely

---

[1] He was, as the Indians say, "making his medicine," a term of very elastic meaning.

torn with briers. They are likewise obliged to abstain from any commerce with their women for the like period, the latter restriction being considered as indispensable to their success.

Early in June, Tootoosch,[1] the crazy chief, died. On being acquainted with his death, the whole village, men, women, and children, set up a loud cry, with every testimony of the greatest grief, which they continued for more than three hours. As soon as he was dead, the body, according to their custom, was laid out on a plank, having the head bound round with a red bark fillet, which is with them an emblem of mourning and sorrow. After lying some time in this manner, he was wrapped in an otter-skin robe, and, three fathoms of Ife-whaw being put about his neck, he was placed in a large coffin or box of about three feet deep, which was ornamented on the outside with two rows of the small white shells. In this, the most valuable articles of his property were placed with him, among which were no less than twenty-four prime sea-otter skins.

At night, which is their time for interring the dead, the coffin was borne by eight men with two poles thrust through ropes passed around it, to the place of burial, accompanied by his wife and family, with their hair cut short in token of grief, all the inhabitants joining the procession.

The place of burial was a large cavern on the side of a hill at a little distance from the village, in which, after depositing the coffin carefully, all the attendants repaired to Maquina's house, where a number of articles

---

[1] "Tootoosch" is the Thunder Bird of "Aht" mythology.

belonging to the deceased, consisting of blankets, pieces of cloth, etc., were burned by a person appointed by Maquina for that purpose, dressed and painted in the highest style, with his head covered with white down, who, as he put in the several pieces one by one, poured upon them a quantity of oil to increase the flame, in the intervals between making a speech and playing off a variety of buffoon tricks, and the whole closed with a feast, and a dance from Sat-sat-sok-sis, the king's son.

The man who performed the ceremony of burning on this occasion was a very singular character named Kinneclimmets. He was held in high estimation by the king, though only of the common class, probably from his talent for mimicry and buffoonery, and might be considered as a kind of king's jester, or rather, as combining in his person the character of a buffoon with that of master of ceremonies and public orator to his majesty, as he was the one who at feasts always regulated the places of the guests, delivered speeches on receiving or returning visits, besides amusing the company at all their entertainments, with a variety of monkey pranks and antic gestures, which appeared to these savages the height of wit and humour, but would be considered as extremely low by the least polished people.

Almost all the kings or head chiefs of the principal tribes were accompanied by a similar character, who appeared to be attached to their dignity, and are called in their language *Climmer-habbee.*

This man Kinneclimmets was particularly odious to Thompson, who would never join in the laugh at his

tricks, but when he began, would almost always quit
the house with a very surly look, and an exclama-
tion of "Cursed fool!" which Maquina, who thought
nothing could equal the cleverness of his *Climmer-
habbee*, used to remark with much dissatisfaction, asking
me why Thompson never laughed, observing that I
must have had a very good-tempered woman indeed
for my mother, as my father was so very ill-natured a
man.

Among those performances that gained him the
greatest applause was his talent of eating to excess,
for I have known him devour at one meal no less than
seventy-five large herrings; and at another time, when
a great feast was given by Maquina, he undertook, after
drinking three pints of oil by way of a whet, to eat four
dried salmon, and five quarts of spawn, mixed up with
a gallon of train-oil, and actually succeeded in swallow-
ing the greater part of this mess, until his stomach
became so overloaded as to discharge its contents in
the dish.   One of his exhibitions, however, had nearly
cost him his life; this was on the occasion of Kla-quak-
ee-na, one of the chiefs, having bought him a new wife,
in celebration of which he ran three times through a
large fire, and burned himself in such a manner that he
was not able to stir for more than four weeks.   These
feats of savage skill were much praised by Maquina,
who never failed to make him presents of cloth, muskets,
etc., on such occasions.

The death of Tootoosch increased still more the
disquietude which his delirium had excited among the
savages, and all those chiefs who had killed our men
became much alarmed lest they should be seized with

the same disorder and die like him; more particularly, as I had told Maquina that 1 believed his insanity was a punishment inflicted on him by Quahootze, for his cruelty in murdering two innocent men who had never injured him.

CHAPTER XII

WAR WITH THE A-Y-CHARTS—A NIGHT ATTACK—
PROPOSALS TO PURCHASE THE AUTHOR

OUR situation had now become unpleasant in the extreme. The summer was so far advanced that we nearly despaired of a ship arriving to our relief, and with that expectation almost relinquished the hope of ever having it in our power to quit this savage land. We were treated, too, with less indulgence than before, both Thompson and myself being obliged, in addition to our other employments, to perform the laborious task of cutting and collecting fuel, which we had to bring on our shoulders from nearly three miles' distance, as it consisted wholly of dry leaves, all of which near the village had been consumed.

To add to this, we suffered much abuse from the common people, who, when Maquina or some of the chiefs were not present, would insult us, calling us wretched slaves, asking us where was our Tyee or captain, making gestures signifying that his head had been cut off, and that they would do the like to us; though they generally took good care at such times to keep well out of Thompson's reach, as they had more than once experienced, to their cost, the strength of his fist. This conduct was not only provoking and grating to our feelings in the highest degree, but it convinced us of the ill disposition of these savages towards us, and rendered us fearful lest they might at some time or other persuade or force Maquina and the chiefs to put us to death.

We were also often brought to great distress for the want of provisions, so far as to be reduced to collect a scanty supply of mussels and limpets from the rocks, and sometimes even compelled to part with some of our most necessary articles of clothing in order to purchase food for our subsistence.

This was, however, principally owing to the inhabitants themselves experiencing a great scarcity of provisions this season; there having been, in the first place, but very few salmon caught at Friendly Cove, a most unusual circumstance, as they generally abound there in the spring, which was by the natives attributed to their having been driven away by the blood of our men who had been thrown into the sea, which with true savage inconsistency excited their murmurs against Maquina, who had proposed cutting off our ship. Relying on this supply, they had in the most inconsiderate manner squandered away their winter stock of provisions, so that in a few days after their return it was entirely expended.

Nor were the king and chiefs much more fortunate in their whaling, even after I had furnished Maquina with the improved weapon for that purpose; but four whales having been taken during the season, which closes the last of May, including one that had been struck by Maquina and escaped, and was afterwards

driven on shore about six miles from Nootka in almost
a state of putridity.

These afforded but a short supply to a population,
including all ages and sexes, of no less than fifteen
hundred persons, and of a character so very improvident, that, after feasting most gluttonously whenever a
whale was caught, they were several times, for a week
together, reduced to the necessity of eating but once
a day, and of collecting cockles and mussels from the
rocks for their food.

And even after the cod and halibut fishing commenced, in June, in which they met with tolerable
success, such was the savage caprice of Maquina, that
he would often give us but little to eat, finally ordering us to buy a canoe and fishing implements and
go out ourselves and fish, or we should have nothing.
To do this we were compelled to part with our great-
coats, which were not only important to us as garments, but of which we made our beds, spreading them
under us when we slept. From our want of skill,
however, in this new employ, we met with no success;
on discovering which, Maquina ordered us to remain at
home.

Another thing, which to me in particular proved
an almost constant source of vexation and disgust,
and which living among them had not in the least
reconciled me to, was their extreme filthiness, not
only in eating fish, especially the whale, when in a
state of offensive putridity, but while at their meals,
of making a practice of taking the vermin from their
heads or clothes and eating them, by turns thrusting
their fingers into their hair and into the dish, and

spreading their garments over the tubs in which the provision was cooking, in order to set in motion their inhabitants.[1]

Fortunately for Thompson, he regarded this much less than myself, and when I used to point out to him any instance of their filthiness in this respect, he would laugh and reply, "Never mind, John, the more good things the better." I must, however, do Maquina the justice to state, that he was much neater both in his person and eating than were the others, as was likewise his queen, owing, no doubt, to his intercourse with foreigners, which had given him ideas of cleanliness, for I never saw either of them eat any of these animals, but, on the contrary, they appeared not much to relish this taste in others. Their garments, also, were much cleaner, Maquina having been accustomed to give his away when they became soiled, till after he discovered that Thompson and myself kept ours clean by washing them, when he used to make Thompson do the same for him.

Yet amidst this state of endurance and disappoint-

---

[1] This habit—unfortunately not peculiar to the Indians—is still occasionally indulged in. The reason they give for it is, that when the great flood covered the earth—a tradition that is found among other North-West American Indians—they escaped in their canoes, and had to eat lice for lack of any other food, and now practise it out of gratitude. The superstitious observances of these tribes are so numerous that the merest account of those known would fill a volume. One or two interesting instances may be mentioned :—Thus, in sneezing, there is good luck if the right nostril is alone affected. But if the left, then evil fortune is at hand. When they pare their nails, which is not often, they burn the parings, and if the smoke from them goes straight up, their latter end will be good ; if not, they will go to the place of punishment. They used to regard—and perhaps still regard—the whites not as human beings, but as a sort of demons.

ment, in hearing repeatedly of the arrival of ships at the north and south, most of which proved to be idle reports, while expectation was almost wearied out in looking for them, we did not wholly despond, relying on the mercy of the Supreme Being, to offer up to whom our devotions on the days appointed for His worship was our chief consolation and support, though we were sometimes obliged, by our taskmasters, to infringe upon the Sabbath, which was to me a source of much regret.

We were, nevertheless, treated at times with much kindness by Maquina, who would give us a plenty of the best that he had to eat, and occasionally, some small present of cloth for a garment, promising me that, if any ship should arrive within a hundred miles of Nootka, he would send a canoe with a letter from me to the captain, so that he might come to our release. These flattering promises and marks of attention were, however, at those times when he thought himself in personal danger from a mutinous spirit, which the scarcity of provisions had excited among the natives, who, like true savages, imputed all their public calamities, of whatever kind, to the misconduct of their chief, or when he was apprehensive of an attack from some of the other tribes, who were irritated with him for cutting off the *Boston*, as it had prevented ships from coming to trade with them, and were constantly alarming him with idle stories of vessels that were preparing to come against him and exterminate both him and his people.

At such times, he made us keep guard over him both night and day, armed with cutlasses and pistols, being apparently afraid to trust any of his own men. At one time, it was a general revolt of his people that he apprehended; then three of his principal chiefs, among whom was his elder brother, had conspired to take away his life; and at length he fancied that a small party of Klaooquates, between whom and the Nootkians little friendship subsisted, had come to Nootka, under a pretence of trade, for the sole purpose of murdering him and his family, telling us, probably to sharpen our vigilance, that their intention was to kill us likewise; and so strongly were his fears excited on this occasion, that he not only ordered us to keep near him armed by day, whenever he went out, and to patrol at night before his house while they remained, but to continue the same guard for three days after they were gone, and to fire, at one and at four in the morning, one of the great guns, to let them know, if, as he suspected, they were lurking in the neighbourhood, that he was on his guard.

While he was thus favourably disposed towards us, I took an opportunity to inform him of the ill-treatment that we frequently received from his people, and the insults that were offered us by some of the stranger tribes in calling us white slaves, and loading us with other opprobrious terms. He was much displeased, and said that his subjects should not be allowed to treat us ill, and that if any of the strangers did it, he wished us to punish the offenders with death, at the same time directing us, for our security, to go constantly armed.

This permission was soon improved by Thompson to the best advantage; for a few days after, having gone to the pond to wash some of our clothes, and a blanket for Maquina, several Wickinninish who were then at Nootka came thither, and, seeing him washing the clothes, and the blanket spread upon the grass to dry, they began, according to custom, to insult him, and one of them, bolder than the others, walked over the blanket. Thompson was highly incensed, and threatened the Indian with death if he repeated the offence, but he, in contempt of the threat, trampled upon the blanket, when, drawing his cutlass, without further ceremony, Thompson cut off his head, on seeing which the others ran off at full speed. Thompson then, gathering up the clothes and blanket, on which were the marks of the Indian's dirty feet, and taking with him the head, returned and informed the king of what had passed, who was much pleased, and highly commended his conduct. This had a favourable effect for us, not only on the stranger tribes but the inhabitants themselves, who treated us afterwards with less disrespect.

In the latter part of July, Maquina informed me that he was going to war with the *A-y-charts*,[1] a tribe about

---

[1] The E-cha-chets are not at present recognised as a separate tribe. But there is a large village in Clayoquot Sound on the south end of Wakenninish Island which bears that name. Like many now all but extinct tribes, who have become absorbed into greater ones, the E-cha-chets seem in Jewitt's time to have been more numerous. In Meares's narrative, "Lee-cha-ett" is mentioned as a village of Wakenninish, but this could not have been the same place, for Maquina and Wakenninish were at this period on good terms. The river which the expedition ascended to reach the summer salmon fishing village of the tribe was probably either the Bear or the Onamettis, both of which flow through some swampy ground into the head of Bedwall Arm. But as usual Jewitt exaggerated the distance up which the canoemen paddled. There is no river in Vancouver Island navigable for twenty or thirty miles, and few, even when broken by rapids and falls, quite that length.

fifty miles to the south, on account of some controversy that had arisen the preceding summer, and that I must make a number of daggers for his men, and cheetolths for his chiefs, which having completed, he wished me to make for his own use a weapon of quite a different form, in order to dispatch his enemy by one blow on the head, it being the calculation of these nations, on going to war, to surprise their adversaries while asleep. This was a steel dagger, or more properly a spike, of about six inches long, made very sharp, set at right angles in an iron handle of fifteen inches long, terminating at the lower end in a crook or turn, so as to prevent its being wrenched from the hand, and at the upper in a round knob or head, from whence the spike protruded. This instrument I polished highly, and, the more to please Maquina, formed on the back of the knob the resemblance of a man's head, with the mouth open, substituting for eyes black beads, which I fastened in with red sealing-wax. This pleased him much, and was greatly admired by his chiefs, who wanted me to make similar ones for them, but Maquina would not suffer it, reserving for himself alone this weapon.

When these people have finally determined on war, they make it an invariable practice, for three or four weeks prior to the expedition, to go into the water five or six times a day, when they wash and scrub themselves from head to foot with bushes intermixed with briers, so that their bodies and faces will often be entirely covered with blood. During this severe exercise, they are continually exclaiming, "*Wocash, Quahootze, Teechamme ah welth, wik-etish tau-ilth — Kar sub-*

matemas—Wik-sish to hauk matemas—I ya-ish kah-shittle—As-smootish warich matemas"; which signifies, " Good or great God, let me live—Not be sick—Find the enemy—Not fear him—Find him asleep, and kill a great many of them."

During the whole of this period they have no inter-course with their women, and for a week before setting out, abstain from feasting or any kind of merriment, appearing thoughtful, gloomy, and morose, and for the three last days are almost constantly in the water, both by day and night, scrubbing and lacerating themselves in a terrible manner. Maquina, having informed Thompson and myself that he should take us with him, was very solicitous that we should bathe and scrub our-selves in the same way with them, telling me that it would harden our skins, so that the weapons of the enemy would not pierce them, but as we felt no great inclination to amuse ourselves in this manner, we declined it.

The expedition consisted of forty canoes, carrying from ten to twenty men each. Thompson and myself armed ourselves with cutlasses and pistols, but the natives, although they had a plenty of European arms, took with them only their daggers and cheetolths, with a few bows and arrows, the latter being about a yard in length, and pointed with copper, mussel-shell, or bone ; the bows are four feet and a half long, with strings made of whale sinew.

To go to A-y-chart, we ascended, from twenty to thirty miles,[1] a river about the size of that of Tashees, the banks of which are high and covered with wood.

----

[1] This is an exaggerated estimate.

13

At midnight we came in sight of the village, which was situated on the west bank near the shore, on a steep hill difficult of access, and well calculated for defence. It consisted of fifteen or sixteen houses, smaller than those at Nootka, and built in the same style, but compactly placed. By Maquina's directions, the attack was deferred until the first appearance of dawn, as he said that was the time when men slept the soundest.

At length, all being ready for the attack, we landed with the greatest silence, and, going around so as to come upon the foe in the rear, clambered up the hill, and while the natives, as is their custom, entered the several huts creeping on all-fours, my comrade and myself stationed ourselves without to intercept those who should attempt to escape or come to the aid of their friends. I wished, if possible, not to stain my hands in the blood of any fellow-creature; and though Thompson would gladly have put to death all the savages in the country, he was too brave to think of attacking a sleeping enemy.

Having entered the houses, on the war-whoop being given by Maquina as he seized the head of the chief and gave him the fatal blow, all proceeded to the work of death. The A-y-charts, being thus surprised, were unable to make resistance, and, with the exception of a very few who were so fortunate as to make their escape, were all killed, or taken prisoners on condition of becoming slaves to their captors. I had the good fortune to take four captives, whom Maquina, as a favour, permitted me to consider as mine, and occasionally employ them in fishing for me. As for Thompson, who thirsted for revenge, he had no wish to take any

prisoners, but with his cutlass, the only weapon he
would employ against them, succeeded in killing seven
stout fellows who came to attack him, an act which
obtained him great credit with Maquina and the chiefs,
who after this held him in much higher estimation, and
gave him the appellation of " Chehiel-suma-har," it being
the name of a very celebrated warrior of their nation in
ancient times, whose exploits were the constant theme
of their praise.

After having put to death all the old and infirm of
either sex, as is the barbarous practice of these people,
and destroyed the buildings, we re-embarked with our
booty in our canoes for Nootka, where we were received
with great demonstrations of joy by the women and
children, accompanying our war - song with a most
furious drumming on the houses. The next day a great
feast was given by Maquina in celebration of his victory,
which was terminated, as usual, with a dance by Sat-
sat-sok-sis.[1]

Repeated applications had been made to Maquina by
a number of kings or chiefs to purchase me, especially
after he had showed them the harpoon I had made for
him, which he took much pride in, but he constantly
refused to part with me on any terms. Among these,
the king of the Wickinninish was particularly solicitous
to obtain me, having twice applied to Maquina for that
purpose, once in a very formal manner, by sending his
messenger with four canoes, who, as he approached the
shore, decorated in their highest style, with the white
down on his head, etc., declared that he came to buy

---

[1] This is one of the best descriptions of West Coast warfare with which
I am acquainted.

"Tooteyoohannis," the name by which I was known to them, for his master, and that he had brought for that purpose four young male slaves, two highly ornamented canoes, such a number of the skins of metamelth, and of the *quartlack*,[1] or sea-otter, and so many fathoms of cloth and of Ife-whaw, while, as he mentioned the different articles, they were pointed out or held up by his attendants; but even this tempting offer had no influence on Maquina, who in the latter part of the summer was again very strongly urged to sell me by Ulatilla, or, as he is generally called, Machee Ulatilla, chief of the Klaizzarts,[2] who had come to Nootka on a visit.

This chief, who could speak tolerable English, had much more the appearance of a civilised man than any of the savages that I saw. He appeared to be about thirty, was rather small in his person, but extremely well formed, with a skin almost as fair as that of an European, good features, and a countenance expressive of candour and amiableness, and which was almost always brightened with a smile. He was much neater both in his dress and person than any of the other chiefs, seldom wearing paint, except upon his eyebrows, which, after the custom of his country, were plucked out, and a few strips of the pelpelth on the lower part of his face. He always treated me with much kindness, was fond of conversing with me in English and in his own language, asking me many questions relative to my country, its manners, customs, etc., and appeared to take a strong

---

[1] "Quiaotluk," Jewitt, with innate cockneyism, inserting an *r* after *a* wherever this is possible. No Indian can pronounce *r*, any more than a Chinaman can.

[2] Klahosahts.

interest in my fate, telling me that if he could persuade Maquina to part with me, he would put me on board the first ship that came to his country, a promise which, from his subsequent conduct, I have good reason to think he would have performed, as my deliverance at length from captivity and suffering was, under the favour of Divine Providence, wholly owing to him, the only letter that ever reached an European or American vessel out of sixteen that I wrote at different times and sent to various parts of the coast, having been delivered by him in person. So much pleased was I with this man's behaviour to me while at Nootka, that I made for him a cheetolth, which I burnished highly, and engraved with figures. With this he was greatly delighted. I also would have made for him a harpoon, would Maquina have consented.

With hearts full of dejection and almost lost to hope, no ship having appeared off Nootka this season, did my companion and myself accompany the tribe on their removal in September to Tashees, relinquishing in consequence for six months even the remotest expectation of relief.

CHAPTER XIII

MARRIAGE OF THE AUTHOR — HIS ILLNESS — DIS-
MISSES HIS WIFE—RELIGION OF THE NATIVES—
CLIMATE

SOON after our establishment there, Maquina informed
me that he and his chiefs had held council both before
and after quitting Nootka, in which they had determined that I must marry one of their women, urging as
a reason to induce me to consent, that, as there was
now no probability of a ship coming to Nootka to
release me, that I must consider myself as destined
to pass the remainder of my life with them, that the
sooner I conformed to their customs the better,
and that a wife and family would render me more
contented and satisfied with their mode of living. I
remonstrated against this decision, but to no purpose, for he told me that, should I refuse, both
Thompson and myself would be put to death; telling
me, however, that if there were none of the women
of his tribe that pleased me, he would go with me to
some of the other tribes, where he would purchase
for me such a one as I should select. Reduced to
this sad extremity, with death on the one side and
matrimony on the other, I thought proper to choose

what appeared to me the least of the two evils, and consent to be married, on condition that, as I did not fancy any of the Nootka women, I should be permitted to make choice of one from some other tribe.

This being settled, the next morning by daylight, Maquina, with about fifty men in two canoes, set out with me for Ai-tiz-zart,[1] taking with him a quantity of cloth, a number of muskets, sea-otter skins, etc., for the purchase of my bride. With the aid of our paddles and sails, being favoured with a fair breeze, we arrived some time before sunset at the village. Our arrival excited a general alarm, and the men hastened to the shore, armed with the weapons of their country, making many warlike demonstrations, and displaying much zeal and activity. We, in the meantime, remained quietly seated in our canoes, where we remained for about half an hour, when the messenger of the chief, dressed in their best manner, came to welcome us and invite us on shore to eat.[2] We followed him in procession to the chief's house, Maquina at our head, taking care to leave a sufficient number in the boats to protect the property. When we came to the house, we were ushered in with much ceremony, and our respective seats pointed out to us, mine being next to Maquina by his request.

After having been regaled with a feast of herring spawn and oil, Maquina asked me if I saw any among the women who were present that I liked. I immediately

[1] Ayhuttisaht, also in Nootka Sound.
[2] This is the custom if the visit of the strangers has not been announced in advance.

pointed out to a young girl of about seventeen, the daughter of Upquesta, the chief, who was sitting near him by her mother. On this, Maquina, making a sign to his men, arose, and, taking me by the hand, walked into the middle of the room, and sent off two of his men to bring the boxes containing the presents from the canoes. In the meantime, Kinneclimmets, the master of ceremonies, whom I have already spoken of, made himself ready for the part he was to act, by powdering his hair with white down. When the chests were brought in, specimens of the several articles were taken out, and showed by our men, one of whom held up a musket, another a skin, a third a piece of cloth, etc.

On this Kinneclimmets stepped forward, and, addressing the chief, informed him that all these belonged to me, mentioning the number of each kind, and that they were offered to him for the purchase of his daughter Eu - stoch - ee - exqua, as a wife for me. As he said this, the men who held up the various articles walked up to the chief, and with a very stern and morose look, the complimentary one on these occasions, threw them at his feet. Immediately on which, all the tribe, both men and women, who were assembled on this occasion, set up a cry of *Klack-ko-Tyee*,[1] that is, " Thank ye, chief."

His men, after this ceremony, having returned to their places, Maquina rose, and, in a speech of more than half an hour, said much in my praise to the Aitiz-zart chief, telling him that I was as good a man as themselves, differing from them only in being white,

[1] *Ooshyuksomayts* is another expression meaning much the same thing.

that I was besides acquainted with many things of which they were ignorant; that I knew how to make daggers, cheetolths, and harpoons, and was a very valuable person, whom he was determined to keep always with him; praising me at the same time for the goodness of my temper, and the manner in which I had conducted myself since I had been with them, observing that all the people of Nootka, and even the children, loved me.

While Maquina was speaking, his master of ceremonies was continually skipping about, making the most extravagant gestures, and exclaiming " *Wocash!* " When he had ceased, the Ai-tiz-zart chief arose, amidst the acclamations of his people, and began with setting forth the many good qualities and accomplishments of his daughter; that he loved her greatly, and as she was his only one, he could not think of parting with her. He spoke in this manner for some time, but finally concluded by consenting to the proposed union, requesting that she might be well used and kindly treated by her husband. At the close of the speech, when the chief began to manifest a disposition to consent to our union, Kinneclimmets again began to call out as loud as he could bawl, " *Wocash!* " cutting a thousand capers and spinning himself around on his heel like a top.

When Upquesta had finished his speech, he directed his people to carry back the presents which Maquina had given him, to me, together with two young male slaves to assist me in fishing. These, after having been placed before me, were by Maquina's men taken on board the canoes. This ceremony being over, we were invited by one of the principal chiefs to a feast at his house, of *Klussamit,*[1] or dried herring, where, after the eating was over, Kinneclimmets amused the company very highly with his tricks, and the evening's entertainment was closed by a new war-song from our men, and one in return from the Ai-tiz-zarts, accompanied with expressive gestures, and wielding of their weapons.

After this our company returned to lodge at Upquesta's, except a few who were left on board the canoes to watch the property. In the morning I received from the chief his daughter, with an earnest request that I would use her well, which I promised him; when, taking leave of her parents, she accompanied me with apparent satisfaction on board of the canoe.

The wind being ahead, the natives were obliged to have recourse to their paddles, accompanying them with their songs, interspersed with the witticisms and buffoonery of Kinneclimmets, who, in his capacity of king's steersman, one of his functions which I forgot to enumerate, not only guided the course of the canoe, but regulated the singing of the boatmen. At about five in the morning we reached Tashees, where we found all the inhabitants collected on the shore to receive us.

We were welcomed with loud shouts of joy, and exclamations of "*Wocash!*" and the women, taking my bride under their charge, conducted her to Maquina's house, to be kept with them for ten days; it being

---

[1] *Kloosmit* is "herring" (*Meletta cærulea*) generally. *Klooshist* is dried salmon, a more common article of food.

an universal custom, as Maquina informed me, that no intercourse should take place between the new married pair during that period. At night Maquina gave a great feast, which was succeeded by a dance, in which all the women joined, and thus ended the festivities of my marriage.[1]

The term of my probation being over, Maquina assigned me as an apartment the space in the upper part of his house between him and his elder brother, whose room was opposite. Here I established myself with my family, consisting of myself and wife, Thompson, and the little Sat-sat-sok-sis, who had always been strongly attached to me, and now solicited his father to let him live with me, to which he consented.

This boy was handsome, extremely well formed, amiable, and of a pleasant, sprightly disposition. I used to take a pleasure in decorating him with rings, bracelets, ear-jewels, etc., which I made for him of copper, and ornamented and polished them in my best manner. I was also very careful to keep him free from vermin of every kind, washing him and combing his hair every day. These marks of attention were not only very pleasing to the child, who delighted in being kept neat and clean, as well as in being dressed off in his finery, but was highly gratifying both to Maquina and his queen, who used to express much satisfaction at my care of him.

In making my domestic establishment, I determined,

[1] Jewitt's marriage was less ceremonious than is usual with Indians of any rank, and the ten days' probation was not according to modern customs.

as far as possible, to live in a more comfortable and cleanly manner than the others. For this purpose I erected with planks a partition of about three feet high between mine and the adjoining rooms, and made three bedsteads of the same, which I covered with boards, for my family to sleep on, which I found much more comfortable than sleeping on the floor amidst the dirt.

Fortunately, I found my Indian princess both amiable and intelligent, for one whose limited sphere of observation must necessarily give rise to but a few ideas. She was extremely ready to agree to anything that I proposed relative to our mode of living, was very attentive in keeping her garments and person neat and clean, and appeared in every respect solicitous to please me.

She was, as I have said, about seventeen; her person was small but well formed, as were her features; her complexion was, without exception, fairer than any of the women, with considerable colour in her cheeks, her hair long, black, and much softer than is usual with them, and her teeth small, even, and of a dazzling whiteness; while the expression of her countenance indicated sweetness of temper and modesty. She would indeed have been considered as very pretty in any country, and, excepting Maquina's queen, was by far the handsomest of any of their women.

With a partner possessing so many attractions, many may be apt to conclude that I must have found myself happy,—at least, comparatively so; but far otherwise was it with me. A compulsory marriage with the most beautiful and accomplished person in the world can never prove a source of real happiness; and, in my situation, I could not but view this connection as a chain that was to bind me down to this savage land, and prevent my ever again seeing a civilised country; especially when, in a few days after, Maquina informed me that there had been a meeting of his chiefs, in which it had been determined that, as I had married one of their women, I must be considered as one of them, and conform to their customs, and that in future neither myself nor Thompson should wear our European clothes, but dress in kutsaks[1] like themselves. This order was to me most painful, but I persuaded Maquina at length so far to relax in it as to permit me to wear those I had at present, which were almost worn out, and not to compel Thompson to change his dress, observing that, as he was an old man, such a change would cause his death.

Their religious celebration, which the last year took place in December, was in this commenced on the 15th of November, and continued for fourteen days. As I was now considered as one of them, instead of being ordered to the woods, Maquina directed Thompson and myself to remain and pray with them to Quahootze to be good to them, and thank him for what he had done.

It was opened in much the same manner as the former. After which, all the men and women in the

---

[1] *Kutsak*, or *kotsack*, or *kootsick*, or *cotsack*, for all these forms occur, was the blanket worn cloakwise, rendered familiar to Europeans in so many pictures and sketches.

village assembled at Maquina's house, in their plainest dresses, and without any kind of ornaments about them, having their heads bound around with the red fillet, a token of dejection and humiliation, and their countenances expressive of seriousness and melancholy. The performances during the continuance of this celebration consisted almost wholly in singing a number of songs to mournful airs, the king regulating the time by beating on his hollow plank or drum, accompanied by one of his chiefs seated near him with the great rattle. In the meantime they ate but seldom, and then very little, retiring to sleep late, and rising at the first appearance of dawn, and even interrupting this short period of repose by getting up at midnight and singing.

The ceremony was terminated by an exhibition of a similar character to the one of the last year, but still more cruel. A boy of twelve years old, with six bayonets run into his flesh, one through each arm and thigh, and through each side close to the ribs, was carried around the room suspended upon them, without manifesting any symptoms of pain. Maquina, on my inquiring the reason of this display, informed me that it was an ancient custom of his nation to sacrifice a man at the close of this solemnity, in honour of their God, but that his father had abolished it, and substituted this in its place.[1] The whole closed on the evening of

[1] Human sacrifices are quite common among the Northern tribes. But in Vancouver they were very rare in my time, and are now still less frequent. In 1863 the burial of a chief was celebrated by the heads of several tribesmen being fixed about his grave. These were not taken by force, but surrendered by the trembling tribesmen, the victims being most

the 29th, with a great feast of salmon spawn and oil, at which the natives, as usual, made up for their late abstinence.

A few days after, a circumstance occurred, which, from its singularity, I cannot forbear mentioning. I was sent for by my neighbour Yealthlower, the king's elder brother, to file his teeth, which operation having been performed, he informed me that a new wife, whom he had a little time before purchased, having refused to sleep with him, it was his intention, provided she persisted in her refusal, to bite off her nose. I endeavoured to dissuade him from it, but he was determined, and, in fact, performed his savage threat that very night, saying that since she would not be his wife, she should not be that of any other, and in the morning sent her back to her father.

The inhuman act did not, however, proceed from any innate cruelty of disposition or malice, as he was far from being of a barbarous temper; but such is the despotism exercised by these savages over their women, that he no doubt considered it as a just punishment for

likely slaves. In 1788, Meares affirms, on what we believe to be insufficient evidence, that Maquina (Moqulla) sacrificed a human being every new moon, to gratify "his unnatural appetite" for human flesh. The victim was a slave selected by the blindfolded chief catching him in a house in which a number were assembled. Meares even declares that Maquina acknowledged his weakness, and that though Callicum, another chief, avoided cannibalism, he reposed on a pillow filled with human skulls. If so, the practice has ceased. Yet cannibalism was undeniably practised at times among the Indians of both the East and West coasts. There were in 1866 Indians living in Koskeemo Sound, who still talked of the delights of human flesh. Many years ago, the Bella-Bellas ate a servant of the Hudson Bay Company, and the Nuchaltaws of Cape Mudge are affirmed by old traders to have paid the same doubtful compliment to a sailor who fell into their clutches.

her offence, in being so obstinate and perverse; as he afterwards told me, that in similar cases the husband had a right with them to disfigure his wife in this way or some other, to prevent her ever marrying again.

About the middle of December, we left Tashees for Cooptee. As usual at this season, we found the herrings in great plenty, and here the same scene of riotous feasting that I witnessed last year was renewed by our improvident natives, who, in addition to their usual fare, had a plentiful supply of wild geese, which were brought us in great quantities by the Eshquates. These, as Maquina informed me, were caught with nets made from bark in the fresh waters of that country. Those who take them make choice for that purpose of a dark and rainy night, and, with their canoes stuck with lighted torches, proceed with as little noise as possible to the place where the geese are collected, who, dazzled by the light, suffer themselves to be approached very near, when the net is thrown over them, and in this manner from fifty to sixty, or even more, will sometimes be taken at one cast.

On the 15th of January 1805, about midnight, I was thrown into considerable alarm, in consequence of an eclipse of the moon, being awakened from my sleep by a great outcry of the inhabitants. On going to discover the cause of this tumult, I found them all out of their houses, bearing lighted torches, singing and beating upon pieces of plank; and when I asked them the reason of this proceeding, they pointed to the moon, and said that a great cod-fish was en-

INDIAN CHIEF'S GRAVE (TEMP. 1863).

14

deavouring to swallow her, and that they were driving him away. The origin of this superstition I could not discover.

Though, in some respects, my situation was rendered more comfortable since my marriage, as I lived in a more cleanly manner, and had my food better and more neatly cooked, of which, besides, I had always a plenty, my slaves generally furnishing me, and Upquesta never failing to send me an ample supply by the canoes that came from Ai-tiz-zart; still, from my being obliged at this season of the year to change my accustomed clothing, and to dress like the natives, with only a piece of cloth of about two yards long thrown loosely around me, my European clothes having been for some time entirely worn out, I suffered more than I can express from the cold, especially as I was compelled to perform the laborious task of cutting and bringing the firewood, which was rendered still more oppressive to me, from my comrade, for a considerable part of the winter, not having it in his power to lend me his aid, in consequence of an attack of the rheumatism in one of his knees, with which he suffered for more than four months, two or three weeks of which he was so ill as to be under the necessity to leave the house.

This state of suffering, with the little hope I now had of ever escaping from the savages, began to render my life irksome to me; still, however, I lost not my confidence in the aid of the Supreme Being, to whom, whenever the weather and a suspension from the tasks imposed on me would permit, I never failed regularly on Sundays to retire to the wood to worship, taking Thompson with me when he was able to go.

On the 20th of February, we returned to our summer quarters at Nootka, but on my part, with far different sensations than the last spring, being now almost in despair of any vessel arriving to release us, or our being permitted to depart if there should.

Soon after our return, as preparatory to the whaling season, Maquina ordered me to make a good number of harpoons for himself and his chiefs, several of which I had completed, with some lances, when, on the 16th of March, I was taken very ill with a violent colic, caused, I presume, from having suffered so much from the cold, in going without proper clothing. For a number of hours I was in great pain, and expected to die, and on its leaving me, I was so weak as scarcely to be able to stand, while I had nothing comforting to take, nor anything to drink but cold water.

On the day following, a slave belonging to Maquina died, and was immediately, as is their custom in such cases, tossed unceremoniously out of doors, from whence he was taken by some others and thrown into the water. The treatment of this poor creature made a melancholy impression upon my mind, as I could not but think that such probably would be my fate should I die among these heathens, and so far from receiving a decent burial, that I should not even be allowed the common privilege of having a little earth thrown over my remains.

The feebleness in which the violent attack of my disorder had left me, the dejection I felt at the almost hopelessness of my situation and the want of warm clothing and proper nursing, though my Indian wife, as far as she knew how, was always ready, even solicitous, to do everything for me she could, still kept me very much indisposed, which Maquina perceiving, he finally told me that if I did not like living with my wife, and that was the cause of my being so sad, I might part with her. This proposal I readily accepted, and the next day Maquina sent her back to her father.

On parting with me she discovered much emotion, begging me that I would suffer her to remain till I had recovered, as there was no one who would take so good care of me as herself. But when I told her she must go, for that I did not think I should ever get well, which in truth I but little expected, and that her father would take good care of her and treat her much more kindly than Maquina, she took an affectionate leave, telling me that she hoped I should soon get better, and left her two slaves to take care of me.

Though I rejoiced at her departure, I was greatly affected with the simple expressions of her regard for me, and could not but feel strongly interested for this poor girl, who in all her conduct towards me had discovered so much mildness and attention to my wishes; and had it not been that I considered her as an almost insuperable obstacle to my being permitted to leave the country, I should no doubt have felt the deprivation of her society a real loss. After her departure, I requested Maquina that, as I had parted with my wife, he would permit me to resume my

European dress, as, otherwise, from not having been accustomed to dress like them, I should certainly die. To this he consented, and I once more became comfortably clad.

Change of clothing, but, more than all, the hopes which I now began to indulge that in the course of the summer I should be able' to escape, in a short time restored me to health, so far that I could again go to work in making harpoons for Maquina, who probably, fearing that he should have to part with me, determined to provide himself with a good stock.

I shall not, however, long detain the reader with a detail of occurrences that intervened between this period and that of my escape, which, from that dull uniformity that marks the savage life, would be in a measure but a repetition, nor dwell upon that mental torture I endured from a constant conflict of hope and fear, when the former, almost wearied out with repeated disappointment, offered to our sinking hearts no prospect of release but death, to which we were constantly exposed from the brutal ignorance and savage disposition of the common people, who, in the various councils that were held this season to determine what to do with us in case of the arrival of a ship, were almost always for putting us to death, expecting by that means to conceal the murder of our crew and to throw the blame of it on some other tribe.   These barbarous sentiments were, however, universally opposed by Maquina and his chiefs, who would not consent to our being injured.   But, as some of their customs and traits of national character which I think deserving of notice have not been mentioned, I shall proceed to give an account of them.

The office of king or chief is, with those people, hereditary, and descends to the eldest son, or, in failure of male issue, to the elder brother, who in the regal line is considered as the second person in the kingdom. At feasts, as I have observed, the king is always placed in the highest or seat of honour, and the chiefs according to their respective ranks, which appear in general to be determined by their affinity to the royal family; they are also designated by the embellishments of their mantles or kutsaks. The king, or head *Tyee*, is their leader in war, in the management of which he is perfectly absolute. He is also president of their councils, which are almost always regulated by his opinion. But he has no kind of power over the property of his subjects, nor can he require them to contribute to his wants, being in this respect no more privileged than any other person. He has, in common with his chiefs, the right of holding slaves, which is not enjoyed by private individuals, a regulation probably arising from their having been originally captives taken in battle, the spoils of war being understood as appertaining to the king, who receives and apportions them among his several chiefs and warriors according to their rank and deserts.

In conformity with this idea, the plunder of the *Boston* was all deposited in Maquina's house, who distributed part of it among his chiefs, according to their respective ranks or degree of favour with him, giving to one three hundred muskets, to another one hundred and fifty, with other things in like proportion. The king is, however, obliged to support his dignity by making frequent entertainments, and whenever he receives a large supply of provision, he must invite all the men of his tribe to his house to eat it up, otherwise, as Maquina told me, he would not be considered as conducting himself like a *Tyee*, and would be no more thought of than a common man.

With regard to their religion.—They believe in the existence of a Supreme Being, whom they call *Quahootze*, and who, to use Maquina's expression, was one great *Tyee* in the sky, who gave them their fish, and could take them from them, and was the greatest of all kings. Their usual place of worship appeared to be the water, for whenever they bathed, they addressed some words in form of prayer to the God above, entreating that he would preserve them in health, give them good success in fishing, etc. These prayers were repeated with much more energy on preparing for whaling or for war, as I have already mentioned.

Some of them would sometimes go several miles to bathe, in order to do it in secret; the reason for this I could never learn, though I am induced to think it was in consequence of some family or private quarrel, and that they did not wish what they said to be heard; while at other times they would repair in the same secret manner to the woods to pray. This was more particularly the case with the women, who might also have been prompted by a sentiment of decency to retire for the purpose of bathing, as they are remarkably modest.

I once found one of our women more than two miles from the village on her knees in the woods, with her eyes shut and her face turned towards heaven, uttering words in a lamentable tone, amongst which I distinctly heard, *Wocash Ah - welth*, meaning " good Lord," and which has nearly the same signification with Quahootze.

Though I came very near her, she appeared not to notice me, but continued her devotions. And I have frequently seen the women go alone into the woods, evidently for the purpose of addressing themselves to a superior Being, and it was always very perceptible on their return when they had been thus employed, from their silence and melancholy looks.

They have no belief, however, in a state of future existence, as I discovered in conversation with Maquina at Tootoosch's death, on my attempting to convince him that he still existed, and that he would again see him after his death; but he could comprehend nothing of it, and, pointing to the ground, said that there was the end of him, and that he was like that.[1] Nor do they believe in ghosts, notwithstanding the case of Tootoosch would appear to contradict this assertion,

---

[1] This, in common with other statements of the kind, is more than doubtful. The best account of their religion is by Mr. Sproat, but even he acknowledges that, after two years devoted to the subject, and to the questioning of others who had passed half a lifetime amongst the " Ahts," he could discover very little about their faith which could be pronounced indisputably accurate. Even the Indians themselves are by no means at one on the subject, people without a written creed or sacred books being apt to entertain very contradictory ideas on their theological tenets. I endeavoured to fathom some of their beliefs, and I had ample opportunities; but I confess to the difficulty of getting behind these reserved folk, and I did not meet with sufficient success to make the results worth recording.

but that was a remarkable instance, and such a one as had never been known to occur before; yet from the mummeries performed over the sick, it is very apparent that they believe in the agency of spirits, as they attribute diseases to some evil one that has entered the body of the patient. Neither have they any priests, unless a kind of conjurer[1] may be so considered who sings and prays over the sick to drive away the evil spirit.

On the birth of twins, they have a most singular custom, which, I presume, has its origin in some religious opinion, but what it is, I could never satisfactorily learn. The father is prohibited for the space of two years from eating any kind of meat, or fresh fish, during which time he does no kind of labour whatever, being supplied with what he has occasion for from the tribe. In the meantime, he and his wife, who is also obliged to conform to the same abstinence, with their children, live entirely separate from the others, a small hut being built for their accommodation, and he is never invited to any of the feasts, except such as consist wholly of dried provision, where he is treated with great respect, and seated among the chiefs, though no more himself than a private individual.

Such births are very rare among them; an instance of the kind, however, occurred while I was at Tashees the last time, but it was the only one known since the reign of the former king. The father always appeared

---

[1] What Jewitt calls a "conjurer" is more commonly known in these times as a "medicine man," who was, more often than not, a combination nine parts rogue and one part fool.

very thoughtful and gloomy, never associated with the other inhabitants, and was at none of the feasts, but such as were entirely of dried provision, and of this he ate not to excess, and constantly retired before the amusements commenced. His dress was very plain, and he wore around his head the red fillet of bark, the symbol of mourning and devotion. It was his daily practice to repair to the mountain, with a chief's rattle in his hand, to sing and pray, as Maquina informed me, for the fish to come into their waters. When not thus employed, he kept continually at home, except when sent for to sing and perform his ceremonies over the sick, being considered as a sacred character, and one much in favour with their gods.[1]

These people are remarkably healthful, and live to a very advanced age, having quite a youthful appearance for their years.[2] They have scarcely any disease but the colic, their remedy for which is friction, a person rubbing the bowels of the sick violently, until the pain has subsided, while the conjurer, or holy man, is employed, in the meantime, in making his gestures, singing, and repeating certain words, and blowing off the evil spirit, when the patient

[1] This is entirely different from the views that are entertained by other tribes. The tribes speaking the language which prevails from Port San Juan to Comox are so ashamed of twins, that one of the hapless two is almost invariably killed. I do not remember having ever seen a case. Most of the Indian birth notions are very curious.

[2] They are apt to rapidly change from young-looking to old-looking men, without any of that pleasant "Indian summer" so characteristic of people in more civilised communities. But advanced years are not common. In 1864 the oldest man in the little Opechesaht tribe, whose homes are on the Kleecoot River (flowing out of Sproat Lake into the Alberni Inlet), was only sixty, so far as he could make out.

is wrapped up in a bearskin, in order to produce perspiration.

Their cure for the rheumatism, or similar pains, which I saw applied by Maquina in the case of Thompson, to whom it gave relief, is by cutting or scarifying the part affected. In dressing wounds, they simply wash them with salt water, and bind them up with a strip of cloth, or the bark of a tree. They are, however, very expert and successful in the cure of fractured or dislocated limbs, reducing them very dexterously, and, after binding them up with bark, supporting them with blocks of wood, so as to preserve their position.[1]

During the whole time I was among them, but five natural deaths occurred, Tootoosch and his two infant children, an infant son of Maquina, and the slave whom I have mentioned, a circumstance not a little remarkable in a population of about fifteen hundred; and as respects child-birth, so light do they make of it, that I have seen their women, the day after, employed as usual, as if little or nothing had happened.

The Nootkians in their conduct towards each other are in general pacific and inoffensive, and appear by no means an ill-tempered race, for I do not recollect any instance of a violent quarrel between any of the men, or the men and their wives, while I was with them, that of Yealthlower excepted. But when they are in the least

---

[1] Bilious complaints, constipation, dysentery, consumption, fevers and acute inflammatory diseases, and (amongst some tribes, but not amongst the Nootkians), ophthalmia, are common, though rheumatism and paralysis are infrequent. The "diseases of civilisation," it may be added, have been known for many years.

offended, they appear to be in the most violent rage, acting like so many maniacs, foaming at the mouth, kicking and spitting most furiously ; but this is rather a fashion with them than a demonstration of malignity, as in their public speeches they use the same violence, and he is esteemed the greatest orator who bawls the loudest, stamps, tosses himself about, foams, and spits the most.[1]

In speaking of their regulations, I have omitted mentioning that, on attaining the age of seventeen, the eldest son of a chief is considered as a chief himself, and that whenever the father makes a present, it is always done in the name of his eldest son, or, if he has none, in that of his daughter. The chiefs frequently purchase their wives at the age of eight or ten, to prevent their being engaged by others, though they do not take them from their parents until they are sixteen.

With regard to climate, the greater part of the spring, summer, and autumn is very pleasant, the weather being at no time oppressively hot, and the winters uncommonly mild for so high a latitude, at least, as far as my experience went. At Tashees and Cooptee, where we passed the coldest part of the season, the winter did not set in till late in December, nor have I ever yet known the ice, even on the fresh-water ponds, more than two or three

---

[1] This is still true. When sober they indulge in high words, and are fond of teasing the women until they get out of temper ; but a blow is rare. Even the children seldom fall out, the necessity of small communities living together for mutual protection compelling the members to establish a *modus vivendi*. However, when drunk—and in spite of the laws against liquor being sold to them, this is by no means uncommon— they are prone to seek close quarters and act like angry termagants.

inches in thickness, or a snow exceeding four inches in depth ; but what is wanting in snow, is amply made up in rain, as I have frequently known it, during the winter months, rain almost incessantly for five or six days in succession.

CHAPTER XIV

ARRIVAL OF THE BRIG "LYDIA"—STRATAGEM OF THE
AUTHOR—ITS SUCCESS

IT was now past midsummer, and the hopes we had
indulged of our release became daily more faint, for
though we had heard of no less than seven vessels on
the coast, yet none appeared inclined to venture to
Nootka.

The destruction of the *Boston*, the largest, strongest,
and best equipped ship, with the most valuable cargo
of any that had ever been fitted for the North-West
trade, had inspired the commanders of others with
a general dread of coming thither, lest they should
share the same fate; and though in the letters I wrote
(imploring those who should receive them to come
to the relief of two unfortunate Christians who were
suffering among heathen), I stated the cause of the
Boston's capture, and that there was not the least danger
in coming to Nootka, provided they would follow the
directions I laid down, still I felt very little encourage-
ment that any of these letters would come to hand;
when, on the morning of the 19th of July, a day that will
be ever held by me in grateful remembrance of the
mercies of God, while I was employed with Thompson
in forging daggers for the king, my ears were saluted

with the joyful sound of three cannon, and the cries of the inhabitants, exclaiming "*Weena, weena—Mameth-lee!*"—that is, "Strangers—White men!"

Soon after, several of our people came running into the house, to inform me that a vessel under full sail was coming into the harbour. Though my heart bounded with joy, I repressed my feelings, and, affecting to pay no attention to what was said, told Thompson to be on his guard, and not betray any joy, as our release, and perhaps our lives, depended on our conducting ourselves so as to induce the natives to suppose we were not very anxious to leave them. We continued our work as if nothing had happened, when, in a few minutes after, Maquina came in, and, seeing us at work, appeared much surprised, and asked me if did not know that a vessel had come.

I answered in a careless manner, that it was nothing to me. "How, John," said he, "you no glad go board?" I replied that I cared very little about it, as I had become reconciled to their manner of living, and had no wish to go away. He then told me that he had called a council of his people respecting us, and that we must leave off work and be present at it.

The men having assembled at Maquina's house, he asked them what was their opinion should be done with Thompson and myself, now a vessel had arrived, and whether he had not better go on board himself, to make a trade, and procure such articles as were wanted. Each one of the tribe who wished, gave his opinion. Some were for putting us to death, and pretending to the strangers that a different nation had cut off the *Boston*; while others, less barbarous, were for sending us fifteen or twenty miles back into the country, until the departure of the vessel.

These, however, were the sentiments of the common people, the chiefs opposing our being put to death, or injured, and several of them, among the most forward of whom were Yealthlower and the young chief Toowinnakinnish, were for immediately releasing us; but this, if he could avoid it, by no means appeared to accord with Maquina's wishes.

Having mentioned Toowinnakinnish, I shall briefly observe that he was a young man of about twenty-three years old, the only son of Toopeeshottee, the oldest and most respected chief of the tribe. His son had always been remarkably kind and friendly to me, and I had in return frequently made for him daggers, cheetolths, and other things, in my best manner. He was one of the handsomest men among them, very amiable, and much milder in his manners than any of the others, as well as neater both in his person and house, at least his apartment, without even excepting Maquina.

With regard, however, to Maquina's going on board the vessel, which he discovered a strong inclination to do, there was but one opinion, all remonstrating against it, telling him that the captain would kill him or keep him prisoner, in consequence of his having destroyed our ship. When Maquina had heard their opinions, he told them that he was not afraid of being hurt from going on board the vessel, but that he would, however, as it respected that, be guided by John, whom he had always found true. He then turned to me, and asked me if I thought there would be any danger in his going

15

on board. I answered, that I was not surprised at the advice his people had given him, unacquainted as they were with the manners of the white men, and judging them by their own; but if they had been with them as much as I had, or even himself, they would think very different. That he had almost always experienced good and civil treatment from them, nor had he any reason to fear the contrary now, as they never attempted to harm those who did not injure them; and if he wished to go on board, he might do it, in my opinion, with security.

After reflecting a few moments, he said, with much apparent satisfaction, that if I would write a letter to the captain, telling him good of him, that he had treated Thompson and myself kindly since we had been with him, and to use him well, he would go.

It may easily be supposed that I felt much joy at this determination, but, knowing that the least incaution might annihilate all my hopes of escape, was careful not to manifest it, and to treat his going or staying as a matter perfectly indifferent to me. I told him that, if he wished me to write such a letter, I had no objection, as it was the truth, otherwise I could not have done it.

I then proceeded to write the recommendatory letter, which the reader will naturally imagine was of a somewhat different tenor from the one he had required; for if deception is in any case warrantable, it was certainly so in a situation like ours, where the only chance of regaining that freedom of which we had been so unjustly deprived, depended upon it; and I trust that few, even of the most rigid, will condemn me with severity for making use of it, on an occasion which afforded me the only hope of ever more beholding a Christian country, and preserving myself, if not from death, at least from a life of continued suffering.

The letter which I wrote was nearly in the following terms :—

To Captain ———
    of the Brig ———

Nootka, July 19, 1805.

Sir,—The bearer of this letter is the Indian king by the name of Maquina. He was the instigator of the capture of the ship Boston, of Boston, in North America, John Salter, captain, and of the murder of twenty-five men of her crew, the two only survivors being now on shore—Wherefore I hope you will take care to confine him according to his merits, putting in your dead-lights, and keeping so good a watch over him, that he cannot escape from you. By so doing, we shall be able to obtain our release in the course of a few hours.

John R. Jewitt, Armourer of the " Boston,"
for himself, and
John Thompson, Sail-maker of the said ship.

I have been asked how I dared to write in this manner : my answer is, that from my long residence among these people, I knew that I had little to apprehend from their anger on hearing of their king being confined, while they knew his life depended upon my release, and that they would sooner have given up five hundred white men, than have had him injured. This will serve to explain the little apprehension I felt at their menaces afterwards, for otherwise, sweet as liberty was to me, I should hardly have ventured on so hazardous an experiment.

On my giving the letter to Maquina, he asked me to explain it to him. This I did line by line, as he pointed them out with his finger, but in a sense very different from the real, giving him to understand that I had written to the captain that, as he had been kind to me since I had been taken by him, that it was my wish that the captain should treat him accordingly, and give him what molasses, biscuit, and rum he wanted.

When I had finished, placing his finger in a significant manner on my name at the bottom, and eyeing me with a look that seemed to read my inmost thoughts, he said to me, "John, you no lie?" Never did I undergo such a scrutiny, or ever experience greater apprehensions than I felt at that moment, when my destiny was suspended on the slightest thread, and the least mark of embarrassment on mine, or suspicion of treachery on his part, would probably have rendered my life the sacrifice.

Fortunately I was able to preserve my composure, and my being painted in the Indian manner, which Maquina had since my marriage required of me, prevented any change in my countenance from being noticed, and I replied with considerable promptitude, looking at him in my turn, with all the confidence I could muster,—

"Why do you ask me such a question, Tyee? Have you ever known me to lie?"

"No."

"Then how can you suppose I should tell you a lie now, since I have never done it?" As I was speaking, he still continued looking at me with the same piercing eye, but, observing nothing to excite his suspicion, he told me that he believed what I said was true, and that he would go on board, and gave orders to get ready his canoe. His chiefs again attempted to dissuade him, using every argument for that purpose, while his wives crowded around him, begging him on their knees not to trust himself with the white men. Fortunately for my companion and myself, so strong was his wish of going on board the vessel, that he was deaf to their solicitations, and, making no other reply to them than "John no lie," left the house, taking four prime skins with him as a present to the captain.

Scarcely had the canoe put off, when he ordered his men to stop, and, calling to me, asked me if I did not want to go on board with him. Suspecting this as a question merely intended to ensnare me, I replied that I had no wish to do it, not having any desire to leave them.

On going on board the brig, Maquina immediately gave his present of skins and my letter to the captain, who, on reading it, asked him into the cabin, where he gave him some biscuit and a glass of rum, at the same time privately directing his mate to go forward, and return with five or six of the men armed. When they appeared, the captain told Maquina that he was his prisoner, and should continue so, until the two men, whom he knew to be on shore, were released, at the same time ordering him to be put in irons, and the windows secured, which was instantly done, and a couple of men

placed as a guard over him. Maquina was greatly surprised and terrified at this reception ; he, however, made
no attempt to resist, but requested the captain to permit
one of his men to come and see him. One of them was
accordingly called, and Maquina said something to him
which the captain did not understand, but supposed to
be an order to release us, when, the man returning to
the canoe, it was paddled off with the utmost expedition
to the shore.

As the canoe approached, the inhabitants, who had
all collected upon the beach, manifested some uneasi-
ness at not seeing their king on board, but when, on
its arrival, they were told that the captain had made
him a prisoner, and that John had spoke bad about him
in the letter, they all, both men and women, set up a
loud howl, and ran backwards and forwards upon the
shore like so many lunatics, scratching their faces, and
tearing the hair in handfuls from their heads.

After they had beat about in this manner for some
time, the men ran to their huts for their weapons, as if
preparing to attack an invading enemy ; while Maquina's
wives and the rest of the women came around me, and,
throwing themselves on their knees, begged me with
tears to spare his life ; and Sat-sat-sok-sis, who kept
constantly with me, taking me by the hand, wept bitterly,
and joined his entreaties to theirs, that I would not let
the white men kill his father. I told them not to afflict
themselves, that Maquina's life was in no danger, nor
would the least harm be done to him.

The men were, however, extremely exasperated with
me, more particularly the common people, who came
running in the most furious manner towards me,

brandishing their weapons, and threatening to cut me in pieces no bigger than their thumb-nails, while others declared they would burn me alive over a slow fire suspended by my heels. All this fury, however, caused me but little alarm, as I felt convinced they would not dare to execute their threats while the king was on board the brig.

The chiefs took no part in this violent conduct, but came to me, and inquired the reason why Maquina had been thus treated, and if the captain intended to kill him. I told them that if they would silence the people, so that I could be heard, I would explain all to them. They immediately put a stop to the noise, when I informed them that the captain, in confining Maquina, had done it only in order to make them release Thompson and myself, as he well knew we were with them; and if they would do that, their king would receive no injury, but be well treated, otherwise he would be kept a prisoner.

As many of them did not appear to be satisfied with this, and began to repeat their murderous threats— "Kill me," said I to them, "if it is your wish," throwing open the bearskin which I wore. "Here is my breast. I am only one among so many, and can make no resistance ; but unless you wish to see your king hanging by his neck to that pole," pointing to the yard-arm of the brig, "and the sailors firing at him with bullets, you will not do it."

"Oh no," was the general cry, "that must never be ; but what must we do?" I told them that their best plan would be to send Thompson on board, to desire the captain to use Maquina well till I was released, which would be soon. This they were perfectly willing to do, and I directed Thompson to go on board. But he objected, saying that he would not leave me alone with the savages. I told him not to be under any fear for me, for that if I could get him off, I could manage well enough for myself; and that I wished him, immediately on getting on board the brig, to see the captain, and request him to keep Maquina close till I was released, as I was in no danger while he had him safe.

When I saw Thompson off, I asked the natives what they intended to do with me. They said I must talk to the captain again, in another letter, and tell him to let his boat come on shore with Maquina, and that I should be ready to jump into the boat at the same time Maquina should jump on shore. I told them that the captain, who knew that they had killed my shipmates, would never trust his men so near the shore, for fear they could kill them too, as they were so much more numerous, but that if they would select any three of their number to go with me in a canoe, when we came within hail, I would desire the captain to send his boat with Maquina, to receive me in exchange for him.

This appeared to please them, and after some whispering among the chiefs, who, from what words I over-heard, concluded that if the captain should refuse to send his boat with Maquina, the three men would have no difficulty in bringing me back with them, they agreed to my proposal, and selected three of their stoutest men to convey me. Fortunately, having been for some time accustomed to see me armed, and suspecting no design on my part, they paid no attention to the pistols that I had about me.

As I was going into the canoe, little Sat-sat-sok-sis, who could not bear to part with me, asked me, with an affecting simplicity, since I was going away to leave him, if the white men would not let his father come on shore, and not kill him. I told him not to be concerned, for that no one should injure his father, when, taking an affectionate leave of me, and again begging me not to let the white men hurt his father, he ran to comfort his mother, who was at a little distance, with the assurances I had given him.

On entering the canoe, I seated myself in the prow facing the three men, having determined, if it was practicable, from the moment I found Maquina was secured, to get on board the vessel before he was released, hoping by that means to be enabled to obtain the restoration of what property belonging to the *Boston* still remained in the possession of the savages, which I thought, if it could be done, a duty that I owed to the owners. With feelings of joy impossible to be described did I quit the savage shore, confident now that nothing could thwart my escape, or prevent the execution of the plan that I had formed, as the men appointed to convey and guard me were armed with nothing but their paddles.

As we came within hail of the brig, they at once ceased paddling, when, presenting my pistols at them, I ordered them instantly to go on, or I would shoot the whole of them. A proceeding so wholly unexpected threw them into great consternation, and, resuming their paddles, in a few moments, to my inexpressible delight, I once more found myself alongside of a Christian ship, a happiness which I had almost despaired of ever again enjoying. All the crew crowded to the side to see me as the canoe came up, and manifested much joy at my safety. I immediately leaped on board, where I was welcomed by the captain, Samuel Hill, of the brig *Lydia* of Boston, who congratulated me on my escape, informing me that he had received my letter off Kloiz-zart [1] from the chief Machee Ulatilla, who came off himself in his canoe to deliver it to him, on which he immediately proceeded hither to aid me. I returned him my thanks in the best manner I could for his humanity, though I hardly knew what I said, such was the agitated state of my feelings at that moment, with joy for my escape, thankfulness to the Supreme Being who had so mercifully preserved me, and gratitude to those whom He had rendered instrumental in my delivery, that I have no doubt that, what with my strange dress, being painted with red and black from head to foot, having a bear-skin wrapped around me, and my long hair, which I was not allowed to cut, fastened on the top of my head in a large bunch, with a sprig of green spruce, I must have appeared more like one deranged than a rational creature, as Captain Hill afterwards told me that he never saw anything in the form of man look so wild as I did when I first came on board.

The captain then asked me into the cabin, where I found Maquina in irons, with a guard over him. He looked very melancholy, but on seeing me his countenance brightened up, and he expressed his pleasure with the welcome of " *Wocash*, John," when, taking him by the hand, I asked the captain's permission to take off his irons, assuring him that, as I was with him, there was

[1] This seems another variant of Klaosaht.

no danger of his being in the least troublesome. He accordingly consented, and I felt a sincere pleasure in freeing from fetters a man who, though he had caused the death of my poor comrades, had nevertheless always proved my friend and protector, and whom I had requested to be thus treated, only with a view of securing my liberty. Maquina smiled, and appeared much pleased at this mark of attention from me. When I had freed the king from his irons, Captain Hill wished to learn the particulars of our capture, observing that an account of the destruction of the ship and her crew had been received at Boston before he sailed, but that nothing more was known, except that two of the men were living, for whose rescue the owners had offered a liberal reward, and that he had been able to get nothing out of the old man, whom the sailors had supplied so plentifully with grog as to bring him too much by the head to give any information.

I gave him a correct statement of the whole proceeding, together with the manner in which my life and that of my comrade had been preserved. On hearing my story, he was greatly irritated against Maquina, and said he ought to be killed. I observed that, however ill he might have acted in taking our ship, yet that it might perhaps be wrong to judge an uninformed savage with the same severity as a civilised person, who had the light of religion and the laws of society to guide him. That Maquina's conduct in taking our ship arose from an insult that he thought he had received from Captain Salter, and from the unjustifiable conduct of some masters of vessels who had robbed him, and, without provocation, killed a number of his people. Besides, that a regard for the safety of others ought to prevent his being put to death, as I had lived long enough with these people to know that revenge of an injury is held sacred by them, and that they would not fail to retaliate, should we kill their king, on the first vessel or boat's crew that should give them an opportunity; and that, though he might consider executing him as but an act of justice, it would probably cost the lives of many Americans.

The captain appeared to be convinced from what I said of the impolicy of taking Maquina's life, and said that he would leave it wholly with me whether to spare or kill him, as he was resolved to incur no censure in either case. I replied that I most certainly should never take the life of a man who had preserved mine, had I no other reason, but as there was some of the *Boston's* property still remaining on shore, I considered it a duty that I owed to those who were interested in that ship, to try to save it for them, and with that view I thought it would be well to keep him on board till it was given up. He concurred in this proposal, saying, if there was any of the property left, it most certainly ought to be got.

During this conversation Maquina was in great anxiety, as, from what English he knew, he perfectly comprehended the subject of our deliberation; constantly interrupting me to inquire what we had determined to do with him, what the captain said, if his life would be spared, and if I did not think that Thompson would kill him. I pacified him as well as I was able, by telling him that he had nothing to fear from the captain, that he would not be hurt, and that if Thompson wished to kill him, he would not be allowed to do it. He would then remind me that I was indebted to him for my life, and that I ought to do by him as he had done by me. I assured him that such was my intention, and I requested him to remain quiet, and not alarm himself, as no harm was intended him. But I found it extremely difficult to convince him of this, as it accorded so little with the ideas of revenge entertained by them. I told him, however, that he must restore all the property still in his possession belonging to the ship. This he was perfectly ready to do, happy to escape on such terms.

But as it was now past five, and too late for the articles to be collected and brought off, I told him that he must content himself to remain on board with me that night, and in the morning he should be set on shore as soon as the things were delivered. To this he agreed, on condition that I would remain with him in the cabin. I then went upon deck, and the canoe that brought me having been sent back, I hailed the inhabitants and told them that their king had agreed to stay on board till the next day, when he would return, but that no canoes must attempt to come near the vessel during the night, as they would be fired upon. They answered, " *Woho, woho*"—" Very well, very well."

I then returned to Maquina, but so great were his terrors, that he would not allow me to sleep, constantly disturbing me with his questions, and repeating, " John, you know, when you was alone, and more than five hundred men were your enemies, I was your friend, and prevented them from putting you and Thompson to death, and now I am in the power of your friends, you ought to do the same by me." I assured him that he would be detained on board no longer than whilst the property was released, and that as soon as it was done, he would be set at liberty.

At daybreak I hailed the natives, and told them that it was Maquina's order that they should bring off the cannon and anchors, and whatever remained with them of the cargo of the ship. This they set about doing with the utmost expedition, transporting the cannon and anchors by lashing together two of their largest canoes, and covering them with planks, and in the course of two hours they delivered everything on board that I could recollect, with Thompson's and my chest, containing the papers of the ship, etc.

When everything belonging to the ship had been restored, Maquina was permitted to return in his canoe, which had been sent for him, with a present of what skins he had collected, which were about sixty, for the captain, in acknowledgment of his having spared his life, and allowed him to depart unhurt.

Such was also the transport he felt when Captain Hill came into the cabin, and told him that he was at liberty to go, that he threw off his mantle, which consisted of four of the very best skins, and gave it to him as a mark of his gratitude; in return for which the captain presented him with a new greatcoat and hat, with which he appeared much delighted. The captain then desired me to inform him that he should return to that part of the coast in November, and that he wished him to keep what skins he should get, which he would buy of him.

This Maquina promised, saying to me at the same time, "John, you know I shall be then at Tashees, but when you come, make *pow*," which means, fire a gun, "to let me know, and I will come down." When he came to the side of the brig, he shook me cordially by the hand, and told me that he hoped I would come to see him again in a big ship, and bring much plenty of blankets, biscuit, molasses, and rum, for him and his son, who loved me a great deal ; and that he would keep all the furs he got for me, observing at the same time, that he should never more take a letter of recommendation from any one, or ever trust himself on board a vessel unless I was there. Then, grasping both my hands with much emotion, while the tears trickled down his cheeks, he bade me farewell, and stept into the canoe, which immediately paddled him on shore.

Notwithstanding my joy at my deliverance, and the pleasing anticipation I felt of once more beholding a civilised country, and again being permitted to offer up my devotions in a Christian church, I could not avoid experiencing a painful sensation on parting with the savage chief, who had preserved my life, and in general treated me with kindness, and, considering their ideas and manners, much better than could have been expected.

My pleasure was also greatly damped by an unfortunate accident that occurred to Toowinnakinnish. That interesting young chief had come on board in the first canoe in the morning, anxious to see and comfort his king. He was received with much kindness by Captain Hill, from the favourable account I gave of him, and invited to remain on board. As the muskets were delivered, he was in the cabin with Maquina, where was also the captain, who, on receiving them, snapped a number in order to try the locks; unluckily one of them happened to be loaded with swan shot, and, going off, discharged its contents into the body of poor Toowinna-kinnish, who was sitting opposite. On hearing the report, I instantly ran into the cabin, where I found him weltering in his blood, with the captain, who was greatly shocked at the accident, endeavouring to assist him.

We raised him up, and did everything in our power to aid and comfort him, telling him that we felt much grieved at his misfortune, and that it was wholly unintentional; this he told me he was perfectly satisfied of, and while we dressed and bound up his wounds, in the best manner we could, he bore the pain with great calmness, and, bidding me farewell, was put on board one of the canoes and taken on shore, where, after languishing a few days, he expired. To me his misfortune was a source of much affliction, as he had no share in the massacre of our crew, was of a most amiable character, and had always treated me with the greatest kindness and hospitality.

The brig being under weigh, immediately on Maquina's quitting us, we proceeded to the northward, constantly keeping the shore in sight, and touching at various places for the purpose of trading.

Having already exceeded the bounds I had prescribed myself, I shall not attempt any account of our voyage upon the coast, or a description of the various nations we met with in the course of it, among whom were a people of a very singular appearance, called by the sailors the *Wooden-lips*.[1] They have many skins, and the trade is principally managed by their women, who are not only expert in making a bargain, but as dexterous in the management of their canoes as the men are elsewhere.

After a period of nearly four months from our leaving Nootka, we returned from the northward to Columbia River, for the purpose of procuring masts, etc., for our brig, which had suffered considerably in her spars during a gale of wind. We proceeded about ten miles up the river to a small Indian village, where we heard from the inhabitants that Captains Clark and Lewis, from the United States of America, had been there about a fortnight before, on their journey overland, and had left several medals with them, which they showed us.[2] The river at this place is of considerable breadth, and both sides of it from its entrance covered with forests of the very finest pine timber, fir, and spruce, interspersed with Indian settlements.

From this place, after providing ourselves with spars, we sailed for Nootka, where we arrived in the latter part of November.[3] The tribe being absent, the agreed signal

[1] These are doubtless the Hydahs and their kindred, the women of whom insert a wooden or ivory trough in their lower lip.

[2] Lewis and Clark reached the mouth of Columbia River on the 15th of November 1805, and wintered at "Fort Clatsop," as they called their dwelling among the then numerous Clatsop Indians, until the 23rd of March 1806, when they began the return journey. The Indians have long ago vanished from the lower Columbia, the remnant of the Clatsops, and the Chinooks on the opposite side, now wearing out the tribal existence in inland Reservations. But it is still possible to come across one of the medals which the explorers distributed amongst them.

[3] It is clear, therefore, from this statement that Lewis and Clark had left Fort Clatsop much more than a fortnight before the vessel in which Jewitt was arrived there; for it is impossible to suppose that the latter took from

16

was given, by firing a cannon, and in a few hours after a canoe appeared, which landed at the village, and, putting the king on shore, came off to the brig. Inquiry was immediately made by Kinneclimmets, who was one of the three men in the canoe, if John was there, as the king had some skins to sell them if he was. I then went forward and invited them on board, with which they readily complied, telling me that Maquina had a number of skins with him, but that he would not come on board unless I would go on shore for him. This I agreed to, provided they would remain in the brig in the meantime. To this they consented, and the captain, taking them into the cabin, treated them with bread and molasses. I then went on shore in the canoe, notwithstanding the remonstrances of Thompson and the captain, who, though he wanted the skins, advised me by no means to put myself in Maquina's power; but I assured him that I had no fear as long as those men were on board.

As I landed, Maquina came up and welcomed me with much joy: on inquiring for the men, I told him that they were to remain till my return. "Ah, John," said he, "I see you are afraid to trust me, but if they had come with you, I should not have hurt you, though I should have taken good care not to let you go on board of another vessel." He then took his chest of skins, and, stepping into the canoe, I paddled him alongside the brig, where he was received and treated by Captain Hill

April to November to get at spars and make the return voyage to Nootka. But the journal of Lewis and Clark was not published until 1814, so that, when Jewitt wrote, he had no ready means of checking the Indians' statement, though neither he nor his editor seems to have troubled books much.

with the greatest cordiality, who bought of him his skins.
He left us much pleased with his reception, inquiring of
me how many moons it would be before I should come
back again to see him and his son ; saying that he would
keep all his furs for me, and that as soon as my son, who
was then about five months old, was of a suitable age to
take from his mother, he would send for him, and take
care of him as his own.[1]

As soon as Maquina had quitted us, we got under
weigh, and stood again to the northward.   We continued
on the coast until the 11th of August, 1806,[2] when,
having completed our trade, we sailed for China, to the
great joy of all our crew, and particularly so to me.
With a degree of satisfaction that I can ill express,
did I quit a coast to which I was resolved nothing
should again tempt me to return, and as the tops
of the mountains sank in the blue waves of the
ocean, I seemed to feel my heart lightened of an
oppressive load.

We had a prosperous passage to China, arriving at
Macao in December, from whence the brig proceeded
to Canton.   There I had the good fortune to meet a
townsman and an old acquaintance in the mate of an
English East Indiaman, named John Hill, whose father,
a wealthy merchant in Hull in the Baltic trade, was a
next-door neighbour to mine.   Shortly after our arrival,

---

[1] The cavalier manner in which Jewitt abandons his family is quite in
the fur-trader's fashion.   It does not seem that he even asked to see his
Indian "princess!"

[2] If Jewitt's information about the departure of Lewis and Clark from the
Columbia River is even approximately accurate, the date must be wrong by
a year, and the subsequent one quite as far out of the due reckoning.   1806
may be a misprint for 1807.

the captain being on board of an English ship, and mentioning his having had the good fortune to liberate two men of the *Boston's* crew from the savages, and that one of them was named Jewitt, my former acquaintance immediately came on board the brig to see me.

Words can ill express my feelings on seeing him. Circumstanced as I was, among persons who were entire strangers to me, to meet thus in a foreign land with one between whom and myself a considerable intimacy had subsisted, was a pleasure that those alone who have been in a similar situation can properly estimate. He appeared on his part no less happy to see me, whom he supposed to be dead, as the account of our capture had been received in England some time before his sailing, and all my friends supposed me to have been murdered. From this young man I received every attention and aid that a feeling heart interested in the fate of another could confer. He supplied me with a new suit of clothes and a hat, a small sum of money for my necessary expenses, and a number of little articles for sea stores on my voyage to America. I also gave him a letter for my father, in which I mentioned my wonderful preservation and escape through the humanity of Captain Hill, with whom I should return to Boston. This letter he enclosed to his father by a ship that was just sailing, in consequence of which it was received much earlier than it otherwise would have been.

We left China in February 1807, and, after a pleasant voyage of one hundred and fourteen days, arrived at Boston. My feelings on once more finding myself in a Christian country, among a people speaking the same language with myself, may be more readily conceived than expressed. In the post office in that place I found a letter for me from my mother, acknowledging the receipt of mine from China, expressing the great joy of my family on hearing of my being alive and well, whom they had for a long time given up for dead, and requesting me to write to them on receiving her letter, which I accordingly did. While in Boston I was treated with much kindness and hospitality by the owners of the ship *Boston*, Messrs. Francis and Thomas Amory of that place, to whom I feel myself under great obligations for their goodness to me, and the assistance which they so readily afforded a stranger in distress.

APPENDIX

I. The "Boston's" Crew

Names of the Crew of the Ship *Boston*, belonging to Boston in Massachusetts, owned by Messrs. F. and T. Amory, Merchants of that place—All of whom, excepting two, were on the 22nd of March, 1803, barbarously murdered by the savages of Nootka.

John Salter,	of Boston,	Captain.
B. Delouisa,	Ditto,	Chief Mate.
William Ingraham,	of New York,	Second Mate.
Edward Thompson,	of Blyth (England),	Boatswain.
Adam Siddle,	of Hull, ditto,	Carpenter.
Philip Brown,	of Cambridge (Mass.),	Joiner.
John Dorthy,	of Situate, ditto,	Blacksmith.
Abraham Waters,	of Philadelphia,	Steward.
Francis Duffield,	of Penton (England),	Tailor.
John Wilson (blackman)	of Virginia,	Cook.
William Caldwell,	of Boston,	·Seaman.
Joseph Miner,	of Newport,	Ditto.
William Robinson,	of Leigh [1] (Scotland),	Ditto.
Thomas Wilson,	of Air,[2] ditto,	Ditto.
Andrew Kelly,	Ditto, ditto,	Ditto.
Robert Burton,	of the Isle of Man,	Ditto.
James M'Clay,	of Dublin,	Ditto.
Thomas Platten,	of Blackney, Norfolk, Eng.	Ditto.
Thomas Newton,	of Hull, ,,	Ditto.
Charles Bates,	of St. James Deeping, ,,	Ditto.
John Hall,	of Newcastle, ,,	Ditto.
Samuel Wood,	of Glasgow (Scotland),	Ditto.
Peter Alstrom,	Norwegian,	Ditto.
Francis Marten,	Portuguese,	Ditto.
Jupiter Senegal (blackman)		Ditto.
John Thompson,	Philadelphia,	Sail Maker,
		who escaped—since dead.
John R. Jewitt,	of Hull (England),	Armourer,

the writer of the Journal from whence this Narrative is taken, and who at present, March 1815, resides in Middletown, in the State of Connecticut.

[1] Leith.   [2] Ayr.

II. WAR-SONG OF THE NOOTKA TRIBE

Commencing with a Chorus repeated at the end of each line.

Hah-yee hah yar har, he yar hah.
Hah-yah hee yar har—he yar hah.
Iye ie ee yah har—ee yie hah.
Ie yar ee yar hah—ee yar yah.
Ie yar ee I yar yar hah—Ie yar ee yee yah !

Ie-yee ma hi-chill at-sish Kla-ha—Hah-ye-hah.
Que nok ar parts arsh waw—Ie yie-yar.
Waw-hoo naks sar hasch—Yar-hah. I-yar hee I-yar.
Waw hoo naks ar hasch yak-queets sish ni-ese,
Waw har. Hie yee ah-hah.

Repeated over and over, with gestures and brandishing of weapons.

NOTE.

Ie-yee ma hi-chill signifies, '' Ye do not know.'' It appears to be a poetical mode of expression, the common one for '' You do not know '' being *Wik-kum-atash;* from this, it would seem that they have two languages, one for their songs and another for common use. The general meaning of this first stanza appears to be, '' Ye little know, ye men of Klahar, what valiant warriors we are. Poorly can our foes contend with us, when we come on with our daggers,'' etc.

The Nootkians have no songs of an historical nature, nor do they appear to have any tradition respecting their origin.[1]

[1] That is not quite true. They have several of a vague order : one, for example, is that all the Indians are sprung from Quawteaht and the Thunder Birds. Another is that all the tribes on the West Coast come from the west ; the different tribes having sprung from the canoes full of migrants stranded by a storm here and there, and so forth.

III. A LIST OF WORDS

In the Nootkian Language, the most in use.[1]

Check-up,	Man.
Kloots-mah,	Woman.
Noowexa,	Father.
Hooma-hexa,	Mother.
Tanassis,	Child.
Katlahtik,	Brother.
Kloot-chem-up,	Sister.
Tanassis-check-up,	Son.
Tanassis-kloots-mah,	Daughter.
Tau-hat-se-tee,	Head.
Kassee,	Eyes.
Hap-se-up,	Hair.
Neetsa,	Nose.
Parpee,	Ears.
Chee-chee,	Teeth.
Choop,	Tongue.
Kook-a-nik-sa,	Hands.
Klish-klin,	Feet.
Oop-helth,	Sun or Moon.
Tar-toose,	Stars.
Sie-yah,	Sky.
Toop-elth,	Sea.
Cha-hak,	Fresh water.
Meet-la,	Rain.
Queece,	Snow.
Noot-chee,	Mountain or hill.

[1] Most of the words in this vocabulary are given with reasonable correctness, though the transliteration is somewhat primitive. A fuller and more accurate one may be found in the Appendix to Sproat's *Scenes and Studies of Savage Life* (1868), pp. 295-309, so that it is not necessary to annotate the present one. Those in Cook's *Voyage* and in Dawson and Tolmie's *Comparative Vocabularies of the Indian Tribes of British Columbia* (1884), are short and imperfect. I have a much fuller one in manuscript.

Kla-tur-miss, ...	Earth.
Een-nuk-see, ...	Fire or fuel
Mook-see, ...	Rock.
Muk-ka-tee, ...	House.
Wik, ...	No.
He-ho, ...	Yes.
Kak-koelth, ...	Slave.
Mah-hack, ...	Whale.
Klack-e-miss, ...	Oil.
Quart-lak, ...	Sea-otter.
Coo-coo-ho-sa. . . .	Seal.
Moo-watch, ...	Bear.
So-har, ...	Salmon.
Toosch-qua, ...	Cod.
Pow-ee, ...	Halibut.
Kloos-a-mit, ...	Herring.
Chap-atz, ...	Canoe.
Oo-wha-pa, ...	Paddle.
Chee-me-na, ...	Fish-hook.
Chee-men, ...	Fish-hooks.
Sick-a-minny, . . .	Iron.
Toophelth, ...	Cloth.
Cham-mass, ...	Fruit.
Cham-mas-sish, . . .	Sweet or pleasant to the taste.
oot-sus, ...	Powder.
Chee-pokes, ...	Copper.
Hah-welks, ...	Hungry.
Nee-sim-mer-hise, . . .	Enough.
Chat-ta-yek, ...	Knife or dagger.
Klick-er-yek, ...	Rings.
Quish-ar, ...	Smoke.
Mar-met-ta, ...	Goose or duck.
Pook-shit-tle, . . .	To blow.
Een-a-qui-shit-tle, . . .	To kindle a fire.
Ar-teese, ...	To bathe.
Ma-mook-su-mah, . . .	To go to fish.
Smootish-check-up, . .	Warrior.
Cha-alt-see klat-tur wah, . .	Go off, or go away.
Ma-kook, ...	To sell.
Kah-ah-pah-chilt, . . .	Give me something.
Oo-nah, ...	How many.
Iy ah-ish, ...	Much.
Ko-mme-tak, ...	I understand.

I-yee ma hak, ...	I do not understand.
Em-ma-chap, ...	To play.
Kle-whar, ...	To laugh.
Mac-kam-mah-sish, . . .	Do you want to buy.
Kah-ah-coh, ...	Bring it.
Sah-wauk, ...	One.
Att-la, ...	Two.
Kat-sa, ...	Three.
Mooh, ...	Four.
Soo-chah, ...	Five.
Noo-poo, ...	Six.
At-tle-poo, ...	Seven.
At-lah-quelth, ...	Eight.
Saw-wauk-quelth, ...	Nine.
Hy-o, ...	Ten.
Sak-aitz, ...	Twenty.
Soo-jewk, ...	One hundred.
Hy-e-oak, ...	One thousand.

INDEX

MORRISON AND GIBB, PRINTERS, EDINBURGH.

The Investors' Review.

Edited by A. J. WILSON.

MONTHLY, 1s. NET.

Vol. I. (1892) and Vol. II. (1893). *Cloth, 21s. each.* Vol. III.
(January-June 1894), Vol. IV. (July-December 1894), Vol. V.
(January-June 1895), and Vol. VI. (July-December 1895).
Cloth, 7s. 6d. net.

THE INVESTORS' REVIEW is entirely independent. It
deals with all subjects which may affect the value of
investments, social and political, as well as financial.

Besides articles on economic questions and the economic side
of politics, written from original standpoints, the INVESTORS'
REVIEW contains many notes and hints on subjects of current
interest to investors, carefully compiled historical analyses of
individual Joint-Stock Companies, short résumés of the latest
published Company Balance-Sheets, and occasional Critical Notes
on New Investments offered to the public of any plausibility
or importance. These are invariably written from the point of
view of an impartial and experienced observer.

This Review is indispensable to all who desire, not mere market
tips, but the actual truth about public securities. It allows them to
see the inside of London finance with a thoroughness and out-
spokenness no other publication of the kind attempts.

CLEMENT WILSON,
29 PATERNOSTER ROW, LONDON, E.C.

✳

THE HISTORY OF CURRENCY,

1252=1894.

BEING an Account of the Gold and Silver Moneys and Monetary Standards of Europe and America, together with an Examination of the effects of Currency and Exchange Phenomena on Commercial and National Progress and Well-being.

BY WILLIAM A. SHAW, M.A.

Second Edition. Price 15s.

"A valuable addition to economic literature. . . . "—*The Times.*
"L'auteur a rendu un signalé service à la science économique par la publication de son volume."—*Journal des Débats.*
"Mr. Shaw's work possesses a permanent historical interest far transcending the present battle of the standards."—*The N. Y. Nation.*
"There have been few more important contributions to the currency controversy."—*Scotsman.*

BY THE SAME AUTHOR.

Select Tracts and Documents

illustrative of

English Monetary History,

1626-1730.

Comprising Works of

Sir ROBERT COTTON; HENRY ROBINSON; Sir RICHARD TEMPLE and J. S.; Sir ISAAC NEWTON; JOHN CONDUITT; together with Extracts from the Domestic State Papers at H.M. Record Office. Price 6s.

"Mr. Shaw has done the students of currency history a service in publishing this volume."—*Dundee Advertiser.*
"The volume is welcome, both for its illustrations of economic theory and as a contribution to currency history. It need scarcely be said that Mr. Shaw does his editing well."—*Saturday Review.*

CLEMENT WILSON,

29 PATERNOSTER ROW, LONDON, E.C.

A Glossary of Colloquial, Slang, and Technical Terms

IN USE ON THE STOCK EXCHANGE AND IN THE MONEY MARKET.

EDITED BY A. J. WILSON.

This little Work covers more ground than its title implies, since it embraces not only the Language peculiar to the Stock Markets, but often goes beyond that, and offers its Readers valuable counsel.

Price 3s.

"A good deal of useful information is here presented in a very handy form."
—*Times.*

"The work is a most useful one, and admirable in many respects."—*Pall Mall Gazette.*

"The book fills a gap among works of reference."—*Morning Post.*

"A handbook which will no doubt prove useful to a considerable circle."—*Manchester City News.*

"A mastery of its contents should be worth hundreds of pounds to people who have to deal with the Stock Exchange fraternity." —*Manchester Courier.*

"A book that will be found useful in the offices of a large class of business houses."—*Scotsman.*

"The explanations will be found helpful to all who wish to have a clear understanding of the language of the money and stock markets."—*Dundee Advertiser.*

Labour, Socialism, and Strikes.

By YVES GUYOT,

Political Editor of "Le Siècle," formerly Minister of Public Works in France.

With an Introductory Note by A. J. WILSON.

Paper covers, 1s.; cloth, 1s. 6d.

"We would suggest to Socialists that they could find no better theme on which to base their controversial lectures than the declaration of war proclaimed against them by Mr. Guyot."—*Reynolds' Newspaper.*

CLEMENT WILSON,
29 PATERNOSTER ROW, LONDON, E.C.

ROBERT BURNS.

THE POEMS, EPISTLES, SONGS, EPIGRAMS, AND EPITAPHS.

Edited by JAS. A. MANSON.

With Notes, Index, Glossary, and Biographical Sketch.

Price 5s. Two Volumes, small 8vo, cloth, gilt top.

" The biographical sketch is carefully executed, and not too enthusiastic for the occasion."—*Times.*

" Is deserving of notice on account not only of the excellence of its paper and typography, but of the sane way in which the personal character and literary qualities of the author of 'Tam O' Shanter' are appraised in the biographical sketch which serves by way of introduction."—*Daily News.*

" Its price, its completeness, and the care bestowed in the arrangement of its contents, their annotation, and the preparation of a glossary, should have vogue with the admirers of Burns."—*Scotsman.*

" Mr. James A. Manson, the editor, has written a biographical introduction, in which he takes a temperate and common-sense view of the poet."—*Dundee Advertiser.*

" The volumes are such a treat to handle and read that they are certain to be popular."—*Glasgow Herald.*

" To anyone in search of a 'Burns' we thoroughly recommend this scholarly and beautiful edition."—*Freeman's Journal.*

" Contains an admirable biographical sketch, which, unlike most biographies, overlooks with kindly eye the follies of the erratic genius."—*Graphic.*

" There are several features in connection with the work which in our opinion specially commend it to admirers of our national poet at this time. While it is one of the smallest and handiest editions, it is also one of the most complete."—*People's Friend.*

" A most attractive edition."—*Cassell's Saturday Journal.*

" The thoroughness of the notes and the fulness and clearness of the English equivalents in the glossary unite in making this one of the very best editions of Burns ever published."—*North British Daily Mail.*

" A noble edition, which holds its place well with all rivals."—*Irish Times.*

CLEMENT WILSON,
29 PATERNOSTER ROW, LONDON, E.C.

LaVergne, TN USA
18 January 2010
170363LV00002B/61/A